WHAT **NOT** TO WRITE

ASPEN PUBLISHERS

WHAT **NOT** TO WRITE

Real Essays, Real MPTs, Real Feedback

LawTutors
New York Bar Exam
Essay Book

Tania N. Shah, Esq.
President and Founder of LawTutors, LLC

Melissa A. Gill, Esq.
Vice President of LawTutors, LLC

Edited by
Sheri Mason, Esq.

 Wolters Kluwer
Law & Business

AUSTIN   BOSTON   CHICAGO   NEW YORK   THE NETHERLANDS

Aspen Publishers
Attn: Permissions Department
76 Ninth Avenue, 7th Floor
New York, NY 10011-5201

To contact Customer Care, e-mail *customer.care@aspenpublishers.com,* call 1-800-234-1660, fax 1-800-901-9075, or mail correspondence to:

Aspen Publishers
Attn: Order Department
PO Box 990
Frederick, MD 21705

Printed in the United States of America.

1 2 3 4 5 6 7 8 9 0

ISBN 978-0-7355-8813-4

Library of Congress Cataloging-in-Publication Data

Shah, Tania N.
  What not to write: real essays, real MPTs, real feedback / Tania N. Shah, Melissa A. Gill.
    p. cm.
  "LawTutors New York bar exam essay book."
  ISBN 978-0-7355-8813-4
  1. Bar examinations—New York—Study guides. 2. Law—New York—Examinations, questions, etc. 3. Legal composition—Study guides. I. Gill, Melissa A. II. Title.

  KFN5076.S52 2008
  340.076—dc22

                                                                        2009033225

About Wolters Kluwer Law & Business

Wolters Kluwer Law & Business is a leading provider of research information and workflow solutions in key specialty areas. The strengths of the individual brands of Aspen Publishers, CCH, Kluwer Law International and Loislaw are aligned within Wolters Kluwer Law & Business to provide comprehensive, in-depth solutions and expert-authored content for the legal, professional and education markets.

CCH was founded in 1913 and has served more than four generations of business professionals and their clients. The CCH products in the Wolters Kluwer Law & Business group are highly regarded electronic and print resources for legal, securities, antitrust and trade regulation, government contracting, banking, pension, payroll, employment and labor, and healthcare reimbursement and compliance professionals.

Aspen Publishers is a leading information provider for attorneys, business professionals and law students. Written by preeminent authorities, Aspen products offer analytical and practical information in a range of specialty practice areas from securities law and intellectual property to mergers and acquisitions and pension/benefits. Aspen's trusted legal education resources provide professors and students with high-quality, up-to-date and effective resources for successful instruction and study in all areas of the law.

Kluwer Law International supplies the global business community with comprehensive English-language international legal information. Legal practitioners, corporate counsel and business executives around the world rely on the Kluwer Law International journals, loose-leafs, books and electronic products for authoritative information in many areas of international legal practice.

Loislaw is a premier provider of digitized legal content to small law firm practitioners of various specializations. Loislaw provides attorneys with the ability to quickly and efficiently find the necessary legal information they need, when and where they need it, by facilitating access to primary law as well as state-specific law, records, forms and treatises.

Wolters Kluwer Law & Business, a unit of Wolters Kluwer, is headquartered in New York and Riverwoods, Illinois. Wolters Kluwer is a leading multinational publisher and information services company.

Dedication

To Natasha, who always wanted to be a big city gal and always supported my big city dreams.

To Honey, who always made sure I would go to law school, and to Heather, who taught me what not to write once I got there.

Acknowledgments

We would like to acknowledge those people who helped us make this book happen. To Sheri, who came in as our student and is now our NY editor. To Samantha, you were here from the beginning and you keep us in line, and we realize that is no easy task. To Scott, forever loyal. To the entire Aspen staff who believed in this book series and helped make it happen. To our friends Aimee B., Aimee J., Ashley, Katy, Tomas, and Trish for believing in us, encouraging us, and motivating us every step of the way. Most of all, to our families for their unconditional love and support. Finally, to the good Samaritans of New York City, who *literally* picked us up when we fell down.

Contents

WHAT **NOT** TO WRITE

Introduction

Dear Students,

We have to admit, here at LawTutors we *love* that show *What Not to Wear* on TLC and we wondered if we could relay the same message about bar exam essay writing that the producers of the show do about fashion. So, here it is, a tool to help you learn what NOT to write on the bar exam, as well as what TO write. We are also hoping we can be just as entertaining, but we will settle for your learning valuable skills and passing the exam!

WHAT THIS BOOK **IS**

This book is different than any other book on tackling the written portion of the bar exam. First, we show you REAL essays and Multistate Performance Test (MPT) answers: all essays and MPTs in this book are questions from past bar exams, and the answers are actually written by bar candidates. Nothing within the actual essays and MPTs has been changed; even grammar and spelling are kept intact. This gives you an idea of what "good" and "bad" essays and MPTs look like through the eyes of the bar examiners. The only thing that has changed in between what they saw and what you are seeing is the handwriting. We understand that it may be helpful to see the actual handwriting of the exam taker under time pressure, but this is not practical for the purposes of a book. Also, have no fear, all of our students have given us permission to use their answers!

Second, this book shows you that you do not always need a perfect essay or MPT to gain a high score. Oftentimes, our students become overwhelmed by sample answers they see in commercial books; these samples are written by attorneys who use notes and may have an unlimited amount of time. Those samples are not only daunting, but also unobtainable on the actual day of the bar exam. What this book showcases *is* obtainable.

Because we want to show you obtainable answers, we will not be providing model answers. We believe that giving you model answers will not benefit you, as it would be impossible for you to replicate what we can write, with unlimited time and resources, in the amount of time actually allotted for the New York Bar Exam written portion. Therefore, we will only be offering advice and suggestions.

Third, this book is a tool to practice your essays and MPTs and then compare them to the "good" and "bad" answers. We have given you space to write your own critique, and it is to your benefit to think about what is good or bad, and make your own comments. We have found that this approach helps students learn how to write much more than asking leading questions to guide you through your comments. We want you to come to your comments on your own. Obviously, we cannot force you to utilize the space to write your own comments, but it really will help you learn how to write better essays and MPT answers for the New York Bar Exam.

After you have thought about what YOU think, you can flip to what our comments are. These helpful hints tell you exactly why an essay or MPT answer received a high or low score. Notice what is similar in the answers that earned high scores and contrast that with what is similar in the answers that earned low scores.

We realize that your comments might not mirror ours, and that's okay—the goal is to THINK about what makes the answers good and bad. In addition, we also realize that some comments might be redundant, but we hope that rather than have that frustrate you, it will help you see the similarities in all of the bad answers, and the similarities in all of the good answers, so that you may more easily replicate the good answers.

Fourth, we realize that in some cases, you may wonder why a certain essay or MPT got a low score and why a certain essay or MPT got a high score, even though the same issues were spotted in both. This book will show you that two examinees may spot the same type and amount of issues but organize them and express them in ways that make a crucial difference in scoring. This also brings us to the organization of the book. Some students like starting with the lowest scoring essays and going up, building themselves up to the highest scoring essays. Other students have told us they want to see the highest scoring essays first, and then have us end with the lowest scoring essays. However you wish to go through the book is up to you. We have organized it from highest scoring answers in the beginning to lowest scoring answers at the end. If you feel strongly about going through the essays in the reverse, this book makes it easy for you to do that. We have also organized all essays together with a separate section on MPTs at the end.

WHAT THIS BOOK IS **NOT**

This book is *not* like your other essay books.

Frankly, we believe there are a multitude of very helpful books out there on answering the call of the question, outlining your answer, and writing your essay or MPT. We believe that our introduction here is very helpful in tackling these issues, but it is not what our entire book is about. Let's admit it, if you haven't heard a ton of advice on how to write a good essay or MPT by now, you are definitely going to hear it during your bar review studies. There are tried and true published techniques, and we are not worried that you will not get enough exposure to these techniques. What we are worried about is that you will not have enough exposure to *actual written bar exam essays and MPTs*. These speak for themselves, and no amount of technique can give you the type of lessons you learn from actual scored essays.

Hence, the focus of this book is not to teach you substantive law or writing the perfect essay *directly*. The focus of the book mirrors its title: what *not* to write, which is essentially about learning the good from the bad. At the end, you will also learn the good from the good.

We are not writing a book on essays and MPTs by way of a "lecture" format but by way of an "example" format. This is also not a book on substantive law, because we are pretty sure you have one or two or ten of those. While we point out the rules of law, where applicable, in our discussion of the actual essays, we want the student to learn from some of our more general comments and apply them to a multitude of essays; once the student does this, he or she will be prepared to write on *any* essay.

Most of all, we do hope that in addition to learning how to write a great bar exam essay and MPT answer, you have some fun with this book. After all, we had fun writing it.

Sincerely,

Tania N. Shah, Esq.
President and Founder of LawTutors, LLC
www.lawtutors.net
tania.shah@lawtutors.net

Melissa A. Gill, Esq.
Vice President of LawTutors, LLC
melissa.gill@lawtutors.net

The New York Bar Exam

AN INTRODUCTION TO THE NEW YORK BAR EXAM

Like most states, the New York bar exam is a two-day bar exam that consists of one day for New York state–specific law and the Multistate Performance Test (MPT) and one day for the Multistate Bar Examination (MBE). The first day of the exam consists of the following: 5 New York–specific law essay questions, 50 New York–specific law multiple choice questions, and one MPT question, which is a skills test developed by the National Conference of Bar Examiners (NCBE) and discussed later in more detail. To pass the New York bar exam, you must receive a final total weighted scaled score of 665 or higher. Each section is worth a percentage of your total weighted scaled score: the MBE counts for 40 percent of your total score, the five New York essays count for 40 percent, the MPT portion counts for 10 percent, and the state–specific multiple choice counts for the last 10 percent. The New York essays, the New York multiple choice, the MPT, and the MBE are first graded separately. The raw score for each of the four parts is scaled by a predetermined formula and converted to a 0-1000 scale.[1] The scaled score for each part is then multiplied by its weight percentage for the exam. Since New York uses a total weighted scaled score of 665 as its passing mark, a high essay score may offset a lower MBE score, so those of you who have a tougher time scoring high on multiple choice tests may be able to use the essay and MPT portion to your advantage.

So, you might ask, HOW can I do well on the written portion of the exam? Well, we're sure you've heard this before, but it bears repeating: **practice makes perfect**. The more essays you practice writing, the better

---

1. This information is from the NY exam website, http://www.nybarexam.org/TheBar/TheBar.htm#grading.

you will do on exam day. We know it stresses you out to think about writing enough essays to cover *all* the possibly tested subjects (not to mention all those subject's subtopics!). You must keep in mind, however, that to get high scores on the essay section of the bar exam, it's not just *what* you know, but also *how* you write and analyze what you know. In our experience, a combination of writing, outlining, and re-reading essays for each tested subject strengthens your writing and outlining skills while maximizing your exposure to the "types" of essays tested within a subject. We encourage our students to use notes and outlines when writing practice essays, so you are learning the applicable rule AND practicing your writing skills—it's okay to multitask!

It is best to expose yourself to the different types of MPTs that the bar exam may test you on. As with essay questions, practice in outlining, structuring, and writing an MPT are crucial to a well-written answer. Practice as many of these as possible *timed*. You may be great at writing a good memorandum of law, but can you read and analyze hypothetical cases and statutes and write a well-organized memorandum all within 90 minutes? That is the key to the MPT.

FORMAT OF THE NEW YORK WRITTEN PORTION OF THE EXAM

As we said earlier, the first day of the two-day test consists of the written portion of the exam and the New York–specific multiple choice questions. In the morning session you have 3 hours and 15 minutes to complete 3 essays and the 50 New York multiple choice questions. Since you are given all three essays and the multiple choice questions at the same time, you may allocate your time how you wish. However, since each section is weighted differently toward your total weighted scaled score, we recommend that you spend roughly 40 minutes per essay and one hour on the multiple choice section. It is not advisable to spend too much time on one essay or too much time on the multiple choice questions. Because you only have a short amount of time, it is imperative that you have a timing game plan going into the exam.

In the afternoon session, you have three hours to complete the remaining two essays and the one MPT. Like the morning session, you will receive these questions at the same time and may allocate your time how you wish; however, we recommend you spend roughly 90 minutes on the MPT and 45 minutes for each essay.

Tested Areas

You will be expected to be familiar with the law in the following fields:

Agency
Commercial Paper (UCC-3)
Conflict of Laws
Corporations
Domestic Relations
Equitable Remedies
Wills, Trusts and Estates
Federal Jurisdiction
Future Interests
Mortgages
No-Fault Insurance
New York Practice and Procedure
New York Professional Responsibility
Partnership
Personal Property
Secured Transactions (UCC-9)
Trusts
UCC-2
Wills
Workers' Compensation
New York distinctions for the MBE topics

How Is This Different from Every Essay You Have Written in Law School?

You may be thinking that you know how to write essays since you have been doing it for at least three years while in law school. But please note that bar exam essays and MPTs are MUCH different from what you are used to writing for law school.

First and foremost, your professors were testing your knowledge of the law, so it was important to dazzle them with your understanding of case law, dissenting opinions, and the obscure nuances of the law that they taught you. Second, you were NEVER only given 90 minutes in either your writing class or at work to analyze the law and write a memorandum of law. If you were given only 90 minutes, we are sorry—that probably was not fun and even a bit cruel.

For the essays, the bar examiners assume you know the law—after all, you graduated law school. The bar examiners want to see how you apply that law to the facts, so a more minimalist approach is necessary. Putting too much in the essay will not only take up more time than you have, but it will lead the bar examiners to think that you are unsure of yourself and are going in directions that are unnecessary.

Again, unlike law school, where the goal is to test your knowledge of the law, the purpose of the bar exam is to test whether you have the analytical skills to be a lawyer. This means getting straight to the point by analyzing only what is relevant.

For the MPT, the bar examiners give you the law, so they want to see how well you can apply this law by both analyzing it and citing the relevant parts of the law in your discussion.

TEN POINTS ON WRITING THE ESSAY EXAMINATION PART OF THE NEW YORK BAR EXAM

Each state may use a different approach to its written portion of the bar exam. What you need to know about the New York Bar Exam is that it asks *very* specific questions about New York law. This means that there will often be three to five subparts to one essay question. Each subpart is designed to determine how well you can analyze a specific area of the law.

1. *Sit on Your Hands:* We are all guilty of stabbing pen to margins as we read the fact pattern for the first time: today is the day to STOP doing that. Read the fact pattern first like it's a story so you can take everything in. If you start writing issues in the margins right away, you may think the fact pattern is going somewhere it is not and you will waste precious time going down the wrong path. In addition, focus on the call of the question in each subpart before you start outlining issues and only answer what the question is asking. Under no circumstances (and we DO mean this) should you answer a question that is not there.

   The sitting on your hands approach also has another distinct advantage. Sitting on your hands will help prevent you from answering a question before it is asked. By this we mean that some students lose points because they answer MORE than what is being asked by the question and end up answering the second or third subpart to the question before it is asked. For instance, subpart (a) might ask what crimes Bob has committed, while subpart (c) asks about his defenses. Many students are tempted to talk about defenses when discussing Bob's crimes, much the way you would in a law school exam, but this is NOT the question being asked. This is a waste of your time, and will lead the bar examiners to think that you do not follow directions. This is not an ideal first impression.

2. ***Get Straight to the Point:*** In all of the essays that received high points, the examinees spotted the issue, and most often the sub-issue, and they did not address anything other than that one issue asked in the subpart. For example, they will not only spot that the issue is "negligence," but that the particular sub-issue deals with "whether or not the defendant breached a duty of care." The questions are asked in such a way that normally leads you straight to the issue. It is important not to dwell on the "big picture" issues. For example, in many of your law school exams the call of the question at the end of the fact pattern usually asks, "What are the rights and liabilities of the party?" Naturally, you wouldn't want to jump right into talking about breach before you lay out the standard for contract and let the grader know you must determine whether a valid contract exists before getting to the issue of breach. *However, things are different in New York.* The New Yorkers really want you to get to the point and they do not like it if you answer the question in a roundabout way. I'm sure you know never to get a New Yorker upset. Definitely do not get a New York bar examiner upset. Hence, if the question on the New York bar exam asks you about breach of a contract, write about the breach of contract (though you may still want to *think* about whether or not there was a contract, do not *write* about it unless it is part of determining whether or not there was a breach). The questions may often be set up in the form of "rulings" ("did the court rule correctly on determining that there was no breach of contract?" or "Plaintiff challenged the will on the grounds of duress, how should the court rule?"). Remember, stick to the particular issue that the examiner is asking you. One approach is to begin your essay answer by stating the particular (and not the big picture) issue, which you can usually determine from the call of the question. In the latter question, you do not want to spell out all the ways one can challenge a will when they are asking you only about duress.

3. ***The Fact Pattern Is Given to You, There Is No Need to Rewrite It:*** Do not set up a fact section or spend valuable time and space restating what is already in the question. Keep in mind, however, that the facts should be applied as necessary in your analysis. Remember, we told you that this was different from a law school essay and that you want to be more succinct and minimalist. This is one more way to achieve that goal.

4. ***Lay Out the Rules Very Clearly:*** For a well-written New York essay, we suggest that you include a statement of the rule before you apply it to the facts. In all of the essays that received a high score, the rules were spelled out clearly and often even divided into elements. For example, "to prove negligence the plaintiff must prove (i) that the defendant had a duty of care, (ii) that the defendant breached that duty of care, (iii) that the breach of duty was the actual and proximate cause of the injuries, and (iv) that there was an injury. This brings us to our next point. When applicable, cite the source of the relevant law, for instance, "New York EPTL on wills, trusts, probate …" in your rule section. While it is not necessary to waste your time memorizing the various abbreviations and codes, if you know them, include them in your rule section. In addition, it is important to be as precise as possible when outlining the relevant rule. Try not to be vague or overly general.

5. ***Do Not Throw in the Entire Hornbook on Contracts:*** The essays that received high points state the rule in a very clear and *concise* manner. You do not need to state the law in full intricate detail; simply write a sufficiently clear and detailed reference to it so that the examiners do not have to wonder whether you know the law. Only bring up the rule that is relevant to their very specific question. Keep in mind that unlike a law school exam, you should not throw in everything you know about a certain subject. However, the flip side of this is that you should not leave OUT relevant rules. If you think an exception to a rule is relevant, bring up the exception. You will see in certain essays that the way to handle this is to either state ONLY the relevant exception/nuance or to state ALL exceptions or nuances. You never want to only state some of them, as then it appears you are not fully comfortable with the rule.

6. ***Do Not Discuss Issues That Are Not Raised:*** Applying the given facts to the relevant rule in a clear and concise manner is really the key to the New York essay portion of the exam. Avoid sentences that start with "However, if this had happened …" or "If the facts had been different…." The bar examiners give you the facts they want you to use, so do not create new ones. Please.

7. ***New York Nuances:*** A lot of the essays that received high points have relevant references to New York nuances. Knowing the statute of limitations (SOL) is key in New York, as well as understanding New York's No-Fault law. Usually, if there are more than three subparts, one will say something such as "is this action timely?" Here, the examiners want you to talk about SOL and SOL *only*. When we say to be concise, please do not write "yes" or "no" and then get mad at

us because we told you to get straight to the point. This is not cross examination—you still need to explain why you came to that conclusion. For example, you would identify that this is a tort claim, what the SOL is for a tort claim, when the action tolls, and if there are any exceptions that apply here. Many times the issue with the SOL question is when the claim started tolling, so you would want to discuss that as best you can.

8. ***What If I Do Not Know the Law?*** While we of course encourage you to study and learn the law, we know that no bar exam taker is ever going to go into the bar exam and remember everything about New York law. In fact, you will drive yourself crazy if you try. So don't be surprised if there is a question where you just cannot think of the rule or you only have a vague notion of what the rule is. In this instance, you can often rely on your common sense. For example, you may not remember that Joe hitting Sam is a battery but your common sense may tell you that there is probably an issue that Joe hit Sam. You can simply write, "when Joe hit Sam, he committed a tort" or "Sam has a claim against Joe for hitting him." Since you know you must apply the facts in the question to a law, do the best you can instead of skipping it or writing only a one-sentence answer. Discuss the issue as fully as you can so the examiners are not alerted to the fact that you are totally unsure of what is going on. Do not dwell on it and waste precious time or beat yourself up. Again, you don't necessarily need to remember *everything* to do well on the bar exam. You need positive thinking throughout the entire exam, and as you will see, even some high scoring essays missed some key issues. Let us stress that knowing the law, and knowing it well, is always ideal. However, we are realistic in knowing that there will be questions where you just don't remember or know the law. You can still gain a relatively decent score by stating what sounds like a good rule, and a REALLY good analysis.

9. ***Certain Things You Should Never Do on the New York Bar Exam:*** We know you will soon be a big-time New York lawyer and we are almost as excited about this as you are, but in order to get there, here are some things that you just cannot do on the written portion of the exam. Do not write for the sake of writing just because you feel you need to write for 40 minutes straight. Do not be needlessly esoteric or verbose or use really big fancy words that do not have relevance outside of a high scoring verbal section on the SATs. Do not repeat yourself because you feel you were not heard (or "read") clearly enough the first time. You were. Also, on the other hand, do not use be too casual in your writing—it is not appropriate to use

anything that is too colloquial. This is an exam—you are not talking to your best buddy. While the bar exam does not test grammar or a grasp of the English language, it is testing your ability to organize your thoughts and analyze the issue presented—all skills required of a future lawyer. Essentially, this means that the examiners will probably give a higher score to a well-articulated essay than to an essay that is not articulated well even though it covers the same issues.

10. *The Million-Dollar Question: Why Am I Taking the Bar Exam?* Okay, so we did not make the rules, but we can try to shed some light on them. You are now being tested on your ability to apply what you have already learned in law school and to show the bar examiners that you have what it takes to make a great advocate for your clients. Keep that in mind through the entire exam!

HOW TO SPECIFICALLY ANSWER A NEW YORK BAR EXAM ESSAY QUESTION

A well-written essay is one that

1. answers the call of the question;
2. discusses and analyzes the *relevant* issues; and
3. is presented in a concise, logical, and organized way.

Format

1. Read the fact pattern carefully	3-4 minutes
2. Generate an outline and organize an answer	6-8 minutes
3. Write your answer	31-33 minutes
	40-45 minutes

1. Reading the Fact Pattern (3-4 Minutes)

Start by skimming the call of the question to determine what is being asked. Then, read the fact pattern twice—one time like it's a story to quickly determine the subject area(s) that are being tested and then a second time to spot the facts that will help you write your answer. Each line may contain several issues, so be careful when you read. Also, remember that multiple areas of law can and will be tested in one given fact pattern. Pay close attention to the various question subparts, since there will be about three to five. You want to look over the questions you will be answering before starting to think about your answer, so that you know both the limit and the scope of your answer. For instance, one subpart might ask about "what crimes may Bob be charged with," and the next subpart might ask "what defenses might Bob raise." If in subpart (a) you talk about defenses, not only will it alert the bar examiners that you are not reading carefully, you would have already answered subpart (b) and will need to repeat yourself.

2. The Outline (6-8 Minutes)

Why should I outline when I never did before?

Organization is key! Outlining enables you to quickly identify in an orderly fashion all the principles you wish to discuss. Since questions can contain multiple issues, you must practice treating each issue briefly and thoroughly. It is also just as important to plan what NOT to write about, since the question subparts ask specific questions about the fact pattern. It is important to make sure that you address all issues that are relevant, which requires you to think before you write. In addition, as stated above, you will have various subparts, and they will each address separate issues. If you fail to outline, it will be tempting to combine all subparts, which is not ideal and may cost you points on your essay. Outlining will help you decide which issue goes with each subpart.

Do you *know* how much time I have on this exam?

We know: you are pressed for time. We have heard this before many, many times. But we think you will forgive us when we tell you what we are about to say next: outlining really SAVES time in the long run because when you finish outlining you will know exactly what you want to write. In addition, it will keep you organized and prevent you from skipping issues or putting in unnecessary ones. Feel better now?

3. Writing the Answer (31-33 minutes)

Okay, this is the part that the examiners DO see. The stuff you did in the last several minutes is your behind-the-scenes rehearsal. The first thing you must understand is that even though the examiner knows the law, you need to write like the examiner knows nothing about the law. Do not assume the examiner knows anything. The purpose of the exam is to test what YOU know.

Please be legible if you are handwriting the exam. It is hard to grade your answer when the examiner does not know what you are writing. Again, do not be verbose or esoteric; do not be flippant or use slang either.

Example:

"It totally sucks that Jimmy won't get his house. He basically got screwed by his greedy woman." *Please do not do this.*

Example:

"It is quite possible, and perhaps probable, depending on how the outcome of the case will be decided by the family court in Apple County, New York, that the ex-husband, Jimmy in this case, will be denied his ability to enter the premises of 123 Landlocked Lane [hereinafter "property"] and, furthermore, may be required to relinquish his alleged rights to ownership of said aforementioned property in order to conform with the applicable principals of family law, or more generally domestic relations, in this instance and to avenge the alleged and supposed rights of his soon to be ex-wife, Stacey, who claims that aforementioned "property" is now legally within her control, which is also subject to the outcome and interpretation by the family court." *Please do not do this either.*

After you lay out the issue, be sure to lay out the rule in a precise manner. You want to be as clear and detailed as possible, and in addition, lay out any relevant nuances or exceptions. But ONLY if they are relevant.

Finally, keep in mind the bar examiners want to know your conclusion and how you got there, so it is important to put forth a good analysis. Saying things like "if Bob had probable cause" is not answering the question the bar examiners are asking, because more likely than not, they want to know what YOU think of whether Bob had probable cause.

4. About Our Score Range and the Essays We Picked

The essays we chose to include in this book range from a scaled score of 65 to 26.87. They are presented in this book from highest score to lowest score, but you may choose to start with the lowest scored essay before reading the highest scored essay if you wish. It does not make a difference to us and we see logic in doing it both ways.

While you will be writing your own comments and playing "Bar Exam Grader," you should also compare your comments to our comments presented at the end of each essay section.

We chose a wide variety of scores and essays, as well as different essay answers for the same bar question. For example, you may see the same essay question pop up a few times, but the answers and score ranges will all be different. It is important to do comparison comments in your comments section and determine why a certain answer received a higher or lower score. We believe this exercise will really help you decipher the difference between what to write, and what *not* to write. This is because it is easier to see mistakes when others make them, and then avoid them in your own writing!

5. Sample Answers Found on the New York Board of Law Examiners Web Site

The New York Board of Law Examiners posts individual past New York essay questions with sample model answers.[2] These are actually written answers, but they are not perfect answers. Each essay question has two answers posted. We believe that these essays and sample answers will be useful when used in conjunction with this book.

To sum up the essay writing section of this chapter, I think Melissa, my co-author, put it best in a conversation we had several months ago about the New York Bar Exam: *"The main thread I am seeing here is CLEAR, CLEAR, CLEAR; RELEVANT, RELEVANT, RELEVANT; SHORT, SHORT, SHORT! As long as we can convey to our students that they need to CONCISELY, SUCCINTLY, and CLEARLY apply the law to the facts by saying 'here, Bob did this, which satisfied x element' … bada bing, bada bang, bada boom, they are in, they are out, they are New York attorneys!"* Exactly.

WRITING THE MULTISTATE PERFORMANCE TEST PORTION OF THE BAR EXAM

The MPT, developed by the National Conference of Bar Examiners (NCBE), is a 90-minute skills question that requires you to write a legal document. You may be asked to write a motion, a brief, a letter to your client, a memorandum of law, a contract, a closing argument, a complaint, or another legal document such as a will. In addition to the MPT question, you will receive the necessary materials, typically called the Library and File. The File is a hypothetical case file that generally will give you the facts, client correspondence, or additional information that you may find in a client's file. The Library contains the law in the form of cases, statutes, and/or regulations. Keep in mind that the law may not be actual New York law, but may be "made up" law—this is to keep you on your toes! The bar

---

2. See http://www.nybarexam.org/TheBar/TheBar.htm#grading.

examiners will want you to draft your answer according to the law in your MPT Library and not according to existing law.

According to the NCBE:

> The File consists of source documents containing all the facts of the case. The specific assignment the applicant is to complete is described in a memorandum from a supervising attorney. The File might also include, for example, transcripts of interviews, depositions, hearings or trials, pleadings, correspondence, client documents, contracts, newspaper articles, medical records, police reports, and lawyer's notes. Relevant as well as irrelevant facts are included. Facts are sometimes ambiguous, incomplete, or even conflicting. As in practice, a client's or supervising attorney's version of events may be incomplete or unreliable. Applicants are expected to recognize when facts are inconsistent or missing and are expected to identify sources of additional facts.
>
> The Library consists of cases, statutes, regulations and rules, some of which may not be relevant to the assigned lawyering task. The applicant is expected to extract from the Library the legal principles necessary to analyze the problem and perform the task. The MPT is not a test of substantive law, and problems may arise in a variety of fields. Library materials provide sufficient substantive information to complete the task.[3]

Each state using the exam independently grades the MPT and determines the weight allotment. As mentioned before, the MPT is worth 10 percent of the total exam for New York.

Why Are You Taking the MPT?

The MPT is a skills test covering lawyerly-like tasks. Essentially, the examiners want to see your ability to analyze, problem-solve, and organize in a limited amount of time. **In short, they want to know that you will be a good lawyer, and that you have the skills to take a case file and do what it is that lawyers do on a day-to-day basis. This part does not require outside knowledge.**

Guidelines for the MPT

1. Read the directions carefully and follow them.
2. Answer the question asked—do not ramble.
3. Stick to the basic IRAC formula, and do not stray from the expected formula.

---

3. National Conference of Bar Examiners, http://www.ncbex.org/multistate-tests/mpt/mpt-faqs/description1/.

4. Draft the document that is being requested. That means pay attention to the requested audience and tone of the document.
5. Use the law and cases contained in the Library.

Skills Needed for the MPT

Legal Analysis and Reasoning

Just like in law school, here you need to show the bar examiners that you have the ability to identify and formulate legal issues, analyze the relevant legal rules and principles, and apply the RELEVANT (let me stress RELEVANT) facts! This could be in the form of a memo to a supervising attorney, a persuasive memo or brief, a letter to a client, a letter to an opposing counsel, or a letter to an administrative agency.

This includes fact gathering and fact analysis. This means you need to investigate and gather all favorable AND unfavorable facts. Part of your task is to filter out the irrelevant facts in the file and focus only on the things that you need. This is being tested because it is a much-needed skill for a lawyer to have. A client comes into your office and tells you a story—it is up to you to determine what is relevant. Trust us, not everything a client tells you is relevant to the case at hand. You also have to analyze and use the facts—apply them to the relevant statutes and case law available in the Library. Often this means that you should compare and contrast cases with your available facts.

Communication

One of the most important aspects that the MPT tests is your ability to communicate; that is, how well can you express your ideas to a client, senior partner, judge, or opposing counsel? A good attorney is able not only to know and analyze the law but also to effectively convey the law and to explain how it pertains to relevant facts. This means you should be precise and clear, and write to your intended audience. How you write to a client is much different from how you would write to a senior partner or a judge.

Organization

The examiners are testing you on how well you are able to organize your thoughts and analysis in the requested legal document. Can you effectively manage your time and resources? Are you spending the appropriate amount of time on the right issues and rules? Organization is key.

Answer the Question Asked

Be sure to answer the question(s) being asked and ONLY the question(s) being asked. This is key for both your essays AND the MPT. The bar examiners want to know that you will not waste your time delving into irrelevant issues. This is not the time to write a dissertation on the law you know or think you know.

Structure of the MPT Question

1. The File
   a. The Task Memorandum: this is a memo, usually from a supervising attorney, telling you exactly what is to be done. Do not deviate from what your supervising attorney wants from you!
   b. Pointer Memorandum: It is possible that your file may contain a second set of instructions addressing the preferred format of your answer. For example, you may be asked to write interrogatories.
   c. Other Materials: Think about what any client file may contain. There may be notes, a police report, a contract, sketches, or diagrams.
2. The Library: this is basically all the law that you need to perform the task. You should not go beyond the Library for your source of law.

Types of Documents You May Be Asked to Draft

In order of most frequently tested to least frequently tested:
1. ***Persuasive Brief:*** This is a very common MPT task. First and foremost, believe in your client—you are his or her advocate and should always have his or her best interests in mind. While you should be reasonable in your presentation of your analysis, you cannot ethically leave out facts or law that is not favorable to your client. However, your client's situation should always be presented in the best light possible. In your analysis, convince the bar examiner that your position should prevail by emphasizing your client's strong points and minimizing any facts that are not favorable to your client. Begin with your best argument and authorities and convince the court of the strength of your client's position early on, and do not dispose of your opponent's arguments until you have established your position. And, last but not least, always use the facts to make your client look good.

2. **Objective Memorandum:** This is also a very common MPT task and shares popularity with the Persuasive Brief above. While you still need to come to a conclusion in this type of memo, it is a balanced document that is well analyzed and objective.

3. **Opinion Letter:** This is nearly always objective. Here, you are advising the client on the law and the status of her case. If the client is a layperson, write in significantly less of a legal tone. You can cite authorities, but still keep the language to the level that a layperson would understand.

4. **Demand Letter:** This is a letter you usually write to an opposing attorney and is always persuasive. Being persuasive does not mean you need to crush the opposing side with your killer legal self. You can be respectful and still demonstrate confidence in your client's side.

5. **Will, Contract, and Other Documents:** If you are asked to draft one of these, you will always keep the client's goals in mind. Drafting a contract or will, for example, usually requires you to resolve the problems and conflicts that may arise while still meeting the client's goals.

6. **Interrogatories:** These are lists of questions that you are asking the opposing side to answer, so while this is persuasive, keep your tone relatively neutral.

7. **Opening or Closing Arguments:** An opening or closing argument is always persuasive. Element by element, you tell the jury that a theory or ultimate fact in the case has or has not been met and that the elements have or have not been met. This is very fact based, although you may mention the law and the elements that you are trying to prove or disprove. The main thrust of your closing argument should be presenting and interpreting the evidence to support your position.

The Time Factor

You should only spend half your time writing. We will say it again. You should only spend half your time writing. Yes, that is only 45 minutes, and you are given 90 minutes. Why on earth would you spend the other 45 minutes doing stuff that your bar examiner will never see? Because the bar examiner will *know* whether or not you actually took the time to think and organize before you started writing.

So what is the other stuff that you should be doing in the first 45 minutes?

Read the Instructions	1 minute	
The Task Memo	5-7 minutes	Yes, you are reading it a few times to make sure you know exactly what you are supposed to do.
The File	3-5 minutes	
The Library	15 minutes	It may take you some time to get through the law and really understand what authority you are working with.
The File (again)	5-6 minutes	Now that you have read the Library, go back to the File and start spotting the relevant facts that tie into the legal rules you just read over in the Library.
Outlining Your Answer	15 minutes	You must outline. You don't have time *not* to outline. This is essentially your organizational map, to keep you from straying off the path, unable to find your way back. Getting lost is not fun (both on the exam and in real life).
Writing	45 minutes	Now you are ready to write a well-organized, well–thought-out and guided memo, brief, letter, or whatever it is your fictitious supervising attorney from your fictitious law firm wants you to write.

About the MPTs We Picked and the Score Range …

The MPTs you are about to see range in score from highest to lowest; again, you may choose to go from lowest to highest if you wish. Please pay special attention to how the students organized their answers and presented the information in the Library and File. Use the space allotted for your comments and then compare them to the comments we have given for the MPTs.

We would like to stop lecturing you now. Are you ready to try out these techniques yourself? Well, please join us for the rest of the book where we show you what to write, and, more important, what *not* to write.

TORTS *Evaluated in Question 11 As Well*

Driver was traveling west on State Street at 35 miles per hour, the posted speed limit. He entered the intersection of State Street and Main Street without stopping or reducing his speed. Driver's vehicle struck broad-side a car traveling southbound through the intersection on Main Street. Normally, a stop sign would have faced westbound traffic on State Street, but the night before, vandals had stolen the stop sign. Driver was familiar with the intersection, but on this occasion did not observe that the stop sign normally controlling westbound traffic on State Street was not in place. There was no traffic control device for traffic proceeding southbound on Main Street.

Passenger was riding in Driver's vehicle. Although wearing a seat belt, she sustained a fracture to her right arm. Passenger was taken to the hospital following the collision. Physician said that her broken arm did not require surgery and simply placed it in a cast. Three months later, on the day of her last visit to Physician, Passenger was advised that the fracture was not healing, so Passenger decided to change her care from Physician to Surgeon.

Surgeon told Passenger that the type of fracture which Passenger sustained should have been treated differently at the beginning so as to permit proper healing. Surgeon performed a surgical procedure, causing Passenger additional pain and suffering, but also permitting Passenger's fracture to properly heal.

Passenger retained Attorney to represent her interests in any claim against Driver and Physician. Passenger agreed to pay a contingent fee of 1/3 of the amount of any settlement or judgment obtained, after deduction of the expenses of litigation. No writing memorialized this agreement.

Two years and eight months after the accident, Attorney duly commenced an action on Passenger's behalf against Driver and Physician to recover damages for Passenger's pain and suffering. The complaint alleged negligence against Driver and malpractice against Physician.

In answering the complaint, Driver asserted that the accident was not his fault and was unavoidable, and in any event, that the non-healing of the fracture was not caused by the accident. Physician and Driver each raised an affirmative defense based on the statute of limitations.

(a) Was the action timely commenced against each defendant?
(b) Assuming the action was timely commenced as to Driver:
    (1) Analyze the issues relating to the liability of Driver for Passenger's non-economic loss arising from the accident, including a discussion of the merits of Driver's defense that the accident was not his fault and was unavoidable; and
    (2) Analyze the issues relating to the liability of Driver for Passenger's pain and suffering arising from Physician's alleged malpractice.
(c) Will Attorney be entitled to any legal fee for his work on behalf of Passenger if a settlement or judgment is obtained?

Actual Past Bar Exam Answer to Question 1

Score = 64.46

Please Note: You may see typos and grammatical mistakes throughout the examinees' answers in this book, as well as asterisks, which the examinees probably used as a way to mark a sentence for further attention. We have left these in so they match the actual answer given.

a. The issue here is whether the action commenced by passenger against driver was timely commenced. **(1)**

Under NYCPLR **(2)**, a claim for negligence, more specifically, personal injuries in an automobile accident is 3 years.

In this case, the personal injury claim by passenger on driver is timely, since only 2 year and 8 months had elapsed from the time of the accident to the commencement of the action against driver. **(3)** The issue here is whether a cause of action for medical malpractice is time barred, or in the alternative, the action was timely commenced. **(4)** Under the NRCPLR, a medical malpractice cause of action is 2 ½ years from the date of treatment. It should further be noted that under the Continuous Treatment Doctrine, the statute of limitations time frame commences to run at the date of last treatment a patient has sought, regarding the injury. **(5)**

Here, passenger sustained a fracture to her right arm. She went to a physician which told her it was a simple fracture and put it in a case. However, three months after 1st being treated by physician, she was notified that her fracture was not healing, and then went to the surgeon.

Here, passenger commenced an action against physician 2 years and 8 months after the accident. Normally, under the NYCPLR, a medical malpractice cause of action has a statute of limitations of 2 ½ years. However, NYCPLR provides the Continuous Treatment Doctrine, which tolls the cause of action until the treatment for the specific type of injury terminates. **(6)** Here, we are told that passenger, on the last day of her treatment with physician, was told that the fracture was not healing properly. **(7)**

Therefore, under the Continuous Treatment Doctrine, even though the claim was 2 yrs and 8 months after the accident, the claim against physician was timely brought because the statute of limitations was tolled until the last treatment date, which was 2 ½ yrs from the accident, in which a medical malpractice claim is timely brought. **(8)**

b. The issue is what is the liability of a Driver to a passenger's non-economic loss in an automobile accident? And, more specifically, is Diver liable to passenger on the grounds of negligence?

Under the NY Tort Law, the elements of negligence are duty, breach, "but for" and proximate cause, and damages. **(9)** In this case, Driver is liable for passenger under a negligence theory. Here, driver owed passenger a duty of care while driving his car **(10)**, and that he breached this duty when he did not stop at an intersection, where it would normally be a stop sign, and moreover, he did not even slow down. Driver's actions were the factual cause of the accident, because "but for" the driver not stopping at the intersection, he would not have broadsided a car, and would not have gotten into an accident, thereby injuring passenger. Driver's actions were also the proximate cause of passenger's injuries, because passenger's injuries were foreseeable, in that it is foreseeable that this type of injury would occur if Driver did not slow down or stop at an intersection, where normally a stop sign should be. A broken arm is a foreseeable injury resulting from a car accident. The final element to make out a cause of action for negligence is that passenger suffered damages. A broken arm is definitely damages. **(11)**

It should be further noted that in driver is liable for negligence and passenger has a claim. **(12)** Under NY Tort Law, New York also has a no-fault scheme with respect to car accident cases. **(13)** With respect to non-economic losses, the No-Fault laws provide that regardless of the fault, a person's medical bills are paid.

Here, since passenger was injured in Driver's car, passenger's medical expenses will be taken care of by Driver's Insurance policy. In New York, a driver is required to obtain and carry a minimum of a 25,000/50,000 policy of no-fault, also know as PIP insurance, which covers a driver and passengers in a car who is involved in an accident, regardless of fault. The 1st 25,000 covers one person, and the 50,000, covers the rest of the people in the car. A car that has insurance in New York is required to have a 25/50 policy at minimum, and can range up to 175/300 for a private individual, and commercial vehicles have even more, up to $1 million.

In conclusion, under NY's no-fault Laws, for a person to have a claim, it does not matter whose fault the accident is, a person is covered with respect to medical bills.

*It should further be noted that is passenger was in drivers car and driver did not have insurance (which would impose criminal sanctions since it is mandatory under the Laws of the State of New York to carry no-fault insurance), the passenger would be covered under her own automobiles no-fault insurance.

(14) The issue is what injuries constitutes a claim for liability under the NY Tort Laws?

Under the New York UTL and Insurance Laws, in order for a person to have a personal injury claim arising from an automobile accident, more specifically, a claim for injuries, otherwise know as a "BI Claim", an injury must meet "threshold". This is a statute instituted by the State of New York, under the NYS Tort Reform Act, where numerated injuries have potential to bring a claim. These injuries include: death, death of a fetus, dismemberment, fractures, loss of a limb, other injuries such as spinal/cervical/lumbar [sic], and slipped discs, plus loss of work for 90 out of 180 days. A person's injuries must account for one of these factors in order to have a viable claim.

*It should further be noted that a person has 30 days from the date of accident to commence a no-fault claim, and to reserve rights for a "bodily injury claim."

In this case, since there is no other car involved, passenger must put in a claim for no-fault, as well as a bodily injury claim, against drivers insurance. **(15)**

The issue is whether Driver's defense that the accident is not his fault is relevant with respect to NY Insurance No-Fault Laws.

As mentioned above, NY No-fault Law compensate a person's medical expenses with respect to an automobile accident, irregardless whose fault it is.

The claim that passenger stated that Driver was negligent does not matter in a claim for no-fault and medical expenses. The NY Insurance No-Fault laws cover anyone in an accident, so as to limit the number of lawsuits brought into action in automobile accidents. **(16)**

2. **(17)** The issue is can a driver be liable for the negligence of a physician's alleged malpractice?

Under NY Tort Law, a personal is liable for foreseeable injuries due to his negligence. In order to be liable for negligence, there must be a duty, a breach of that duty, "but for" and proximate causation, and damages.

Here, it already has been established that driver owed a duty to passenger, and that he breached that duty when he drove through an intersection.

Further, it should be noted that driver is liable for Passenger's Pain and Suffering arising from Physician's alleged malpractice. It is foreseeable that if a person is in an accident and breaks his arm, that a physician may make a mistake, or otherwise stated, it is foreseeable that a person driving may get into an accident, especially when a person runs through a stop sign, and that a person/passenger may require medical attention. Moreover, it is totally foreseeable **(18)** that a physician may make a mistake, since passengers injuries are the type which could arise out of a car accident. **(19)**

In conclusion, driver will be held responsible for passenger's injuries relating to physicians alleged malpractice.

However, it should be noted that driver can bring a claim against physician for any damages he had to pay out to driver. If the physician was never named in the claim, driver may have a cause of indemnification against physician, in which driver has 6 years from the date of payment to have a cause of action against physician. **(20)** Under NYCPLR, Article 16 also may have an effect on a claim, if passenger asserts a claim against both physician and driver. Driver will be held primarily at fault, whereas physician will be liable for his share as well. Article 16 provides for joint and several liability, which provides for, in the case that we are in NY, and follow a "pure comparative fault/liability," both driver and physician will be liable up to only their proportion of fault for non-economic damage, but will remain liable for 100% of the purely economic damages but as mentioned before, indemnification an contribution are viable remedies.

*It could further be noted that Driver could have sued the city by filing a notice of claim w/in 90 days of the accident, but the claim will not be meritorious because the facts mention that the stop sign was in tact the night before, and the city will argue that they did not have notice. **(21)**
c. The issue is whether an attorney who does not provide his client with a retainer agreement, setting down the fee schedule, is entitled to 1/3 of the settlement of judgment.

Under the NY Rules of Professional Responsibility, a retainer agreement must be signed where contingency fees are agreed upon. This retainer agreement is then memorialized and alluded to in a retained statement, which is then sent up to the NYOCA to obtainer a retainer number, which is used on all closing statements.

Here, since passenger did not sign an agreement, lawyer is not entitled to his contingency fee, unless he is able to show the court some hardship that he was under, which did not allow him to obtain his client's signature.

*However, it should be noted that the above instance can never be proven, and in light of the foregoing, an attorney who breaches his obligation to get a signed retainer agreement is not entitled to his entire legal fee, but only a half of the fee. **(22)**

Your Comments

(1) _____

_____

_____

(2) _____

_____

_____

(3) _____

_____

_____

(4) _____

_____

_____

(5) _____

_____

_____

(6) _____

_____

_____

(7) _____

_____

_____

(8) _____

_____

_____

(9) _____

_____

_____

(10) _____

_____

_____

(11) _____

_____

_____

(12) _____

_____

_____

(13) _____

_____

_____

(14) _____

_____

_____

(15) _____

_____

_____

(16) _____

_____

_____

(17) _____

_____

_____

(18) _____

_____

_____

(19) _____

_____

_____

(20) _____

_____

_____

(21) _____

_____

_____

(22) _____

_____

_____

Our Analysis

(1) Good issue statement. This is always a great start. You want to impress the examiners right from the first sentence.

(2) Bar examiners like it when an examinee adds where the rule comes from. This doesn't mean you have to memorize every statute, but having a general idea of where things come from is always a good idea.

(3) Here, the author laid out the rule clearly and concisely and then very succinctly analyzed it. This is a perfect example of what the examiners would like to see.

(4) This is very awkwardly worded. Do not make things more complicated—keep it simple. See above, where the author laid out a well-worded issue statement.

(5) This is an example of a great rule statement.

(6) The author already stated this in the above paragraph. You are limited for time, so do not be redundant.

(7) Again, the author already stated this. Every time you write a new sentence, ask yourself if you are adding something or merely being repetitive.

(8) This took entirely too long to get to the point. The rule of law and conclusion is correct, but the analysis did not need to be nearly that long. We are being repetitive in stating this, but get to the point and get out. You have no time to be wordy!

(9) This is good. Lay out the issue clearly and then make the rule very clear. The clearer the better!

(10) What was the duty of care? Be sure to clearly analyze every element. Do not assume or leave anything out.

(11) This is an example of a good analysis for a negligence claim. As you can see, the author laid out each element and how the facts applied to each element.

(12) This seems completely out of place. Remember, you do not have time to be repetitive. This was just discussed fully; the author need not bring it up again.

(13) A no fault what? The author probably means insurance, but that is not made clear here.

(14) This would be clearer if the author numbered it b.1. The more organized you can make things, the better.

(15) This one sentence serves as the essay's analysis. The author has laid out an in-depth rule; however, the author never applied the rule to this case. Why is it important that there was only one car involved? The author's statement of the rule doesn't mention anything about the number of cars.

(16) This is all good law, but seems to go into circles and not offer a clear analysis.

(17) This is confusing because there is no "1". This is where outlining will help you, it is important to not get disorganized or confuse the bar examiners!

(18) Do not use words like *totally*. Remember, you are trying to convince the bar examiners that you are a serious attorney, not a Valley girl.

(19) Here is an example of a pretty good analysis.

(20) Remember how you are on a time limit? The question asked about Driver's liability. While claims that Driver may have against Physician may be relevant, it's not a direct answer to the question. This is a good example of something that you may want to mention but not spend a lot of time on.

(21) This seems to stray too far off topic. You have limited time, so stick to the topic at hand.

(22) I'm not sure why this "can never be proven." Is the attorney entitled to nothing for his work? Also, what are the exceptions that would allow the attorney to ask for a non-refundable retainer?

General Comments

Outlining an essay prior to writing will help to organize your thoughts and structure your essay so that all points are mentioned at the appropriate time. As a 60, it's a generally good essay, though it could be higher. It lays out the rules and the issues very well. However, at times the analysis goes in circles and the author goes off in tangents, discussing issues not asked.

CONTRACTS/CORPORATIONS

Evaluated in Questions 5 and 9 as Well

Ana, Bob and Cal were the sole directors and sole shareholders of Feet, Inc., a closely held New York corporation which owned and operated retail shoe stores. Ana, Bob, and Cal each owned 75 shares in the company. On January 2, 2002, Ana, Bob and Cal signed a written shareholders' agreement which provided in pertinent part:

> Upon the death of any shareholder, Feet, Inc. shall, within sixty (60) days of receipt of a written demand from a duly appointed estate representative, purchase the shares of the deceased shareholder for $1,000 per share.

When the agreement was signed, the three directors orally agreed that the buy back provision would apply only if the corporation was making a profit.

In addition to being a director of Feet, Inc., Ana was also a licensed real estate broker and the sole director and shareholder of Ana's Realty, Ltd., a New York corporation. In June 2007, the directors of Feet, Inc., with Ana participating, voted to enter into a contract with Ana's Realty, Ltd. Prior to the vote, Ana disclosed to Bob and Cal that she was the sole shareholder and director of Ana's Realty, Ltd. The vote was two to one with Cal voting against the contract. The written contract provided that if Ana's Realty, Ltd. located a store for Feet Inc. to purchase, Ana's Realty, Ltd. would receive the customary commission of six per cent (6%) of the sales price when title closed. Ana soon found a desirable store at a favorable price, and in October 2007, Feet, Inc. purchased it.

In November 2007, Ana sent a written purchase order to Sal, the president of Shoe Co., and ordered 2,000 pairs of boots, to be delivered to the new store on or about December 1, 2007. The terms of the purchase order called for payment in full upon delivery.

On December 1, 2007, Shoe Co. delivered 2,000 pairs of running shoes to Feet, Inc.'s new store. Ana immediately had the shoes placed in an unlocked storage shed on Feet, Inc.'s property and notified Sal that she was rejecting the shoes. Sal told Ana that the shoes would be picked up within the week. However, three days later the shoes were stolen, and Sal told Ana that he was holding Feet, Inc. responsible for the loss of the shoes.

Cal died in December 2007. On February 1, 2008, Executor was duly appointed as the executor of Cal's estate. Executor gave Ana and Bob a written demand that Feet, Inc. purchase Cal's shares of stock pursuant to the written shareholders' agreement. Bob then informed Executor that Feet Inc. had not made a profit for the past three years, and therefore, the corporation would not buy back Cal's shares. Executor has confirmed that Feet, Inc. has not made a profit for the past three years.

(a) **Is Feet, Inc. liable to Shoe Co. for the loss of the running shoes?**
(b) **Was the contract between Feet, Inc. and Ana's Realty, Ltd. voidable?**
(c) **Is evidence of the oral agreement admissible in an action by Executor to enforce Feet Inc.'s obligation to purchase Cal's shares of stock under the written shareholders' agreement?**

Actual Past Bar Exam Answer to Question 2

Score = 60.96

a) Feet Inc. is liable to Shoe Co.

The issue is whether Feet Inc. is liable to shoe Co because Feet Inc. did not take precautions to safeguard the non-conforming goods until sho co. could pick them up.

The contract here is one for the sale of goods so it is governed by the UCC. **(1)** The UCC requires tender of goods to be conforming on the quantity, quality, and delivery to be as the parties agreed. When, as here both parties are merchants (both buyer and seller have knowledge and work w/goods of the same kind-shoes) a merchant memorandum or purchase order can be used to order goods. When non-conforming goods are tendered, buyer can timely notify the seller of rejection because of the non-conformity and, until the seller can pick up the non conforming goods, the buyer has a duty to take reasonable steps to take care for the goods until the seller can retrieve them. Breach of this duty results in buyer being liable for damages to goods. **(2)** Feet Inc. did not take reasonable steps to safeguard the shoes until shoe Co. could pick up the goods b/c anna placed the shoes in an unlocked storage shed on their property. It is foreseeable that goods placed in an unlocked storage shed will be stolen and therefore it was not reasonable for Ana to think that she was safeguarding them. **(3)**

The shoes were clearly non-conforming since ana ordered boots and Sal delivered shoes **(4)**. Notice was timely given to Seller since the facts state she immediately told Sal of the non-conformity, and sal said he would pick up the shoes within one week which is a reasonable time. Therefore, Ana was under a duty to care for the goods until Sal could pick them up. **(5)**

Ana could be held liable for the damaged goods and may even be deemed to have accepted **(6)** the non-conforming goods since the goods were essentially used inconsistently w/sellers interest by being placed in the unlocked storage. Nevertheless, Ana's duty to care for the non-conforming goods until seller could pick them up breaches her duty and creates liability for Feet Inc. **(7)** Since Ana is a director of Feet Inc., her actions are imputable to Feet Inc thereby creating liability in them. **(8)**

b) The contract is voidable. **(9)** The issue is whether Feet Inc. can void the contract because ana's was an interested director.

Directors to a corporation have the ability to enter contracts on behalf of the corporation for the corporations benefit. Each director has a duty of loyalty to the corporation. Because of this duty, if a director becomes an interested director (has a stake in the contract/some interest in both contracting parties) the corporation must take precautions to prevent the corporations interest. **(10)** If a director is "interested" in a corporation contract, it is not automatic that the contract cannot go forward. If the interested director fully discloses to the other directors her interest/stake in the contract and the contract is fair to the corporation, a majority vote of the board will allow the corporation to enter the contract notwithstanding the director's interest. **(11)**

Here, ana disclosed her interest as director of Ana's Realty to the director's of Feet Inc. and the vote was taken to enter the contract. However, ana participated in the vote. as an interested director she should not have participated in the vote. **(12)** Without her vote there would not have been a majority vote and Feet Inc. would not have contracted w/ana's Realty. Even though the store was purchased at a favorable price, ana voting in her favor (to enter a k with a company she owned) makes the contract voidable. **(13)**

c) The oral agreement is inadmissible.

The issue is whether the buy back provision violated the statute of Frauds. and the Dead Man's statute. **(14)** The statute of Frauds requires writing that is signed by party to be charged in certain instances such as surety contracts, need property contacts, and testamentary dispensation. This requirement exists to prevent perjury of documents. Where a signed writing exists and that writing is initialed by the parties to be a complete and fully integrated embodiment of their agreement, extrinsic evidence cannot be introduced to contradict or even supplement to terms of that writing. This is called the Pond Evidence Rule.

Here, the directors, ana, Bob and cal made an oral agreement that contradicted their written, signed shareholder agreement. Since they equally agreed to buy back shoes if the corporation was making a profit in contrast to their written agreement that did not limit the buy back, the written agreement would prevail as satisfying the statute of frauds and would not be admissible. **(15)**

Ana's contracting would be the Dead Man's Statute which prevents testimony of transactions or contractors w/a decedent. Essentially since decedents lips are sealed so are the lips of those seeking to enforce/prohibit the agreement.

For those reasons, the oral agreement is inadmissible.

Your Comments

(1) _____

_____

_____

(2) _____

_____

_____

(3) _____

_____

_____

(4) _____

_____

_____

(5) _____

_____

_____

(6) _____

_____

_____

(7) _____

_____

_____

(8) _____

_____

_____

(9) _____

_____

_____

(10) _____

_____

_____

(11) _____

_____

_____

(12) _____

_____

_____

(13) _____

_____

_____

(14) _____

_____

_____

(15) _____

_____

_____

Our Analysis

(1) Another example of a great introduction. Impress the examiners right away.

(2) Great explanation of rule. It's very clear and concise.

(3) Please explain why this is relevant. You ALWAYS have to explain the "why." Make sure that your essay has lots of "because" and "when"; otherwise you are not explaining yourself. Do not leave things too conclusory.

(4) Actually, he delivered running shoes. Be careful of misreading facts. This is why taking your time and reading through the essay, so that you understand facts, is so imperative.

(5) Here is a perfect rule explanation and analysis. The author clearly lays out the rule and applies the facts.

(6) This leaves me asking "how so"? You always want to explain yourself. This is key.

(7) This sentence is awkwardly worded, and though it is technically a correct statement, it leads to confusion.

(8) This is all a good analysis.

(9) When drafting an NY essay, you don't always need to follow IRAC. Sometimes, stating your conclusion is a good way to begin. Just be sure to stay consistent. In addition, please do not state the issue twice, since you have limited time.

(10) Good rule statement.

(11) This explanation should be a bit more detailed. It is a bit confusing. How does a majority of the board allow this? We have said this before: explain your statements!

(12) This is inaccurate.

(13) The important fact in this paragraph is that there wasn't a majority of disinterested votes.

(14) The author misses a key issue, which is the Parol Evidence Rule.

(15) This is stated awkwardly. True, the written agreement satisfies the Statute of Frauds requirement that the sale of goods over $500 must be in writing; however, it is the Parol Evidence Rule that would bar admission.

General Comments

It appears to me that the author froze up while answering this essay question, or ran out of time. This can be avoided by outlining your answers. Also, be sure to remember that each subpart is important—the author had a strong answer for the first two subsections, but the last answer may have lost the author some valuable points.

General Comments on Essays That Receive Scores in the 60s

The above essays do a few things really well: they clearly lay out the issues and the rule statements. This is really key to getting a good score. The essays did not score higher because they did not fully analyze everything. However, essays that receive scores in the 60s are still considered "passing," but to be safe, you always want to explain yourself and fully analyze everything you put in your essay.

DOMESTIC RELATIONS

Ann and Jack lived together but never married. In November 2000, Ann became pregnant with Jack's child. After Ann told Jack about her pregnancy, Jack left Ann, saying he wanted nothing to do with the child.

In 2001, while still pregnant, Ann met and married Rick. Shortly thereafter she gave birth to a boy she named Billy, and she listed Rick as Billy's father on the birth certificate. Although Rick knew that Billy was not his biological child, Rick supported Billy and, with Ann's encouragement, treated Billy as his own son. Ann and Rick both held Billy out as Rick's biological child. Billy called Rick "Daddy" and developed close bonds with Rick. Ann never sought or received any child support from Jack. Jack was aware of Billy's birth and, although Jack never doubted that Billy was his biological son, he never made any contact with Billy and did not object to Billy being raised to believe that Rick was his biological parent.

In 2005, after a chance meeting, Jack and Ann decided that they wanted to renew their relationship and raise Billy together. Ann and Rick thereafter separated, and Jack filed a petition seeking a declaration of paternity, establishing that he was Billy's father. Ann did not contest Jack's petition, but Rick, who was permitted to join the proceeding as a respondent, moved to dismiss the petition, asserting that Jack should be estopped from claiming paternity and Ann should be estopped from acquiescing in that claim. A hearing was held at which uncontested proof of the above facts was presented.

After a hearing, the court (1) dismissed Jack's petition on the basis of the doctrine of equitable estoppel.

In 2006, Ann and Rick divorced. The judgment of divorce incorporated but did not merge the terms of a separation agreement entered into by the parties. The separation agreement provided that Rick would be entitled to weekly visitation with Billy and would pay Ann $250 per week in child support, an amount in compliance with the guidelines set forth in the Child Support Standards Act.

In January 2007, Ann began to refuse to permit Rick to have any contact with Billy. Rick continued to attempt to exercise his right to visitation, but Ann actively interfered with all attempts by Rick to see Billy. As a result, Rick stopped paying child support. In July 2007, when he was $5,000 in arrears in child support, Rick moved to cancel the arrears and suspend his obligation to pay child support, in light of Ann's interference with his visitation.

The court (2) granted Rick's motion in all respects. Ann thereafter again began to permit Rick to have visitation with Billy, and Rick resumed paying child support. Rick has now filed a petition seeking a downward modification of his child support obligations. At the hearing on his petition, Rick testified that he was fired from his job as a graphic designer in October 2007 for violating a company policy on computer use. Rick admitted that there are many jobs available in the area consistent with his education and ability, but testified that he applied for several positions and has not been hired.

(a) Were rulings (1) and (2) of the court correct?
(b) How should the court rule on Rick's petition?

Actual Past Bar Exam Answer to Question 3

Score = 59.17

a. 1. The issue is whether equitable estoppel can be used to prevent declaration of paternity.

Biological parents have superior rights over third parties in a child's life. However, when a biological parent **(1)** basically terminates their own parental rights by renouncing a child, having no contact w/a child for six months or more, or does not provide support for that child, rights of a third party may be deemed superior to that of a biological parent. Especially when that third party has provided support, care, is proven as the parent by the child, and that child is held out to the public as that third party's biological child.

Jack, as Billy's biological parent, did not have any contact w/Billy until he was four years old, paid no support for Bill's expenses. Rick on the other hand, as a third party, provided for Billy, treated Billy as his own, held Billy out as his biological son and Billy was even raised to believe Rick was his biological **(2)** father.

Since the goal of equity is to prevent injustice, **(3)** Rick should be deemed Billy's biological father **(4)** and should not be subject to a contest whether Jack is the father. On this other hand, parental rights are protected under substantive due process so this argument may fail rendering dismissal of Jack's petition error.

2. The issue is whether the court has authority to a) cancel child support arrears a b) suspend an obligation to pay child support based on interference w/visitation.

A separation agreement that is incorporation **(5)** but not merged into a divorce decree survives the divorce decree & its terms are controlling since Rick's child support & visitation were terms in the separation agreement, either Rick or Ann's non-compliance is a violation of those terms. Ann's interference w/visitation in violation of the agreement does not permit Rick to stop paying child support. A court is never endowed with discretion to cancel child support already in arrears so the court's order canceling Rick's child support is incorrect. **(6)** A court may suspend a child support obligation if, as here, terms of the agreement are not being complied with. Since the court has discretion to suspend Rick's child support obligation, the ruling is incorrect on that issue. **(7)**

b. The issue is whether losing one's job and inability to obtain another job is a sufficient substantial unanticipated circumstance allowing for downward modification of Rick's support. **(8)** A court has discretion to modify child support if the obligor can assert a substantial change in circumstances. NY presumes that every parent has the means to care for their child so modifying child support, a downward modification at that, requires that an substantial unanticipated circumstances be proven. **(9)** Losing your job is a foreseeable event that a person should anticipate and is not sufficient grounds to modify child support downward. However, Rick may argue that Billy's needs have changed and he does not require as much support, furthermore, with Jack in Billy's life Billy's needs have arguably changed b/c Jack is contributing to Billy's support. These arguments may fail and Rick's loss of employment and inability to procure other employment may not satisfy the unreasonable unanticipated change of circumstances standard for downward modification of support. **(10)**

Your Comments

(1) _____

_____

_____

(2) _____

_____

_____

(3) _____

_____

_____

(4) _____

_____

_____

(5) _____

_____

_____

(6) _____

_____

_____

(7) _____

_____

_____

(8) _____

_____

_____

(9) _____

_____

_____

(10) _____

_____

_____

Our Analysis

(1) This is far too colloquial. Remember at all times that this is a legal exam, not an e-mail to your best friend.

(2) Rule sounds a bit casual, but still works.

(3) Is it to prevent injustice or to help the best interests of the child?

(4) Actually, Rick cannot be deemed Billy's *biological* father since that is based on a blood relationship. Be careful with wording, as the legal profession is a profession of semantics.

(5) Watch grammar; though this is not an English test, you want to make sure you are being clear.

(6) This is a bit disorganized. You also want to make it clear that a parent cannot stop paying child support even if the separation agreement had not merged. This means the obligation to pay support is independent of that agreement. This is not clear from either the rule or analysis that is laid out here.

(7) What would the courts apply? Go into more detail in either the rule or the application or both.

(8) Good issue statement.

(9) Good rule statement.

(10) Structurally, the author did an excellent job of stating a counterargument and whether it would succeed or fail. However, before jumping to Rick's argument, be sure to properly *analyze* the facts with the rule. This is easy to do by applying it back to the facts in the question and stating why. For example, this statement would have been better written if it stated, "Rick's losing his job is a foreseeable event [*why* is it foreseeable?] that he should have anticipated [*why* should he have anticipated it?], and is not sufficient grounds to modify his child support downward."

General Comments

The author should include one statement as to the overall **Conclusion** that Rick's loss of his job would not allow the downward modification of Billy's support. This does not necessarily need to be the last sentence — it's fine if you choose to state your conclusion as your first sentence before your issue.

General Note on IRAC

As you can probably tell, the author is using the **I**ssue **R**ule **A**nalysis Conclusion (IRAC) essay structure. IRAC is one successful method to structure an NY essay. No matter how you structure your essay, the most important paragraph is the analysis paragraph. The author could have expanded on the analysis.

DOMESTIC RELATIONS

Alan and Barbara were married in 1988. They purchased a home as tenants by the entirety, using wedding gift money for the down payment and financing the balance with a mortgage loan. Prior to the marriage, Barbara owned an apartment building known as the Towers. She continued to own the building in her own name following the marriage. From the time of the marriage, Alan helped manage the Towers, splitting the work equally with Barbara.

The couple had two children, Corrine and David. Barbara gave up her job as a dance instructor to take care of the children and the home. She returned to work part time as a receptionist when the younger child entered school. Alan worked as an engineer when the couple met. He received several promotions over the years following the marriage.

In 2006, Barbara commenced a divorce action alleging cruel and inhuman treatment, seeking maintenance and equitable distribution. Barbara's action also seeks custody of both children and child support. David, age 9, has indicated that he wants to live with his father. Alan seeks custody of David, but because Alan does not get along with 14-year-old Corrine, he requests only holiday visits with her. Alan travels frequently for his job, and plans to hire a nanny to help care for David.

The court appointed a law guardian who interviewed the parties and the children. The two children, who are currently living with Barbara under a temporary order of custody, get along well. The law guardian reports that Barbara runs the family household very efficiently as the primary caretaker of the children. The law guardian also reports David has expressed anger toward his mother, primarily because Alan told David that Barbara was seeking to break up the family. The law guardian believes that David's anger toward his mother is temporary and recommends some counseling for David.

At the time of the marriage, the Towers was worth $75,000. It increased in value to $275,000 by the time the divorce action was commenced. All of the appreciation was due to improvements made to the property from the joint and equal efforts and resources of Alan and Barbara. The Towers remains in Barbara's name.

Beginning in 1989, Alan's employer provided a pension plan fully funded by employer contributions. Alan's pension plan account was fully vested and worth $1,000,000 when the divorce action was commenced.

He will not be eligible to receive any funds from the plan until he reaches retirement age in 2017.

The marital home was purchased for $150,000. Due to market conditions only, its value increased to $225,000 by the time the divorce action was commenced. The mortgage on the marital home was fully paid and satisfied in 2005.

(1) How should the court rule regarding the equitable distribution of:
  (a) the Towers, (b) the marital home, and (c) Alan's pension plan account?
(2) How should the court rule regarding custody?
(3) How should the court rule regarding child support?

Actual Past Bar Exam Answer to Question 4

Score = 54.77

1. **(1)** (a) the towers:

The issue is whether the Towers is marital property subject to equitable distribution. In New York, the Domestic Relations Law (DRL) statute governs equitable distribution. Property that spouses owned in their own name before entering the marriage is generally considered non-marital property (i.e. not subject to distribution). **(2)** Barbara owned the Towers prior to the marriage, so the apartment building itself is non-marital property. However, when distributing assets among spouses, the non-monetary efforts of either spouse are considered when determining what is subject to equitable distribution. **(3)** The appreciation ($200,000) of the apartment building is marital property because it was a result of the joint efforts of both spouses. **(4)** The asset accumulated active growth and the increased value is attributed to the work of both Alan and Barbara. **(5)** The building itself ($75,000), however is not marital property, so it is not subject to equitable distribution. **(6)** Therefore, the $275,000 value of the building should be divided as follows:

To Barbara: $75,000 (value of home when marriage began; non-marital property) + half of the accumulate growth ($100,000) = $175,000

To Alan = half of the appreciation of the building's value because of his active efforts in managing the building = $100,000 **(7)**

1. (b) the marital home

The issue is whether the marital home is marital property subject to equitable distribution. In New York, property acquired during the marriage is generally **(8)** considered marital property, regardless of who holds title.

Property received during the marriage to one spouse as a result of inheritance is not subject to equitable distribution. **(9)**

In this case, the home's appreciation in value was passive growth, due to market conditions solely. Therefore, the appreciation is included with value of the home. The house was acquired during the marriage and the spouses took title as tenants by the entirety. The funds were a wedding gift, which is assumed to be given to the spouses equally. Also, both parties were bound by the mortgage since the property was held as tenants by the entirety. When property is held as tenants in the entirety, neither spouse can convey his interest or use it as security without the other spouse. Any mortgage or sale involves both spouses. **(10)**

Accordingly, the marital home is marital property and the value of the house will be divided as follows:

Value of house = $225,000 divided by 2 = $112,500 to each spouse. **(11)**

1. (c) Alan's pension account

The issue is whether Alan's pension account is marital property subject to equitable distribution.

Pension accounts acquired during the marriage are considered marital property, regardless of whose name is on the account. Any amount that has vested during the marriage is subject to equitable distribution. Barbara is entitled to half of the vested amount because of her indirect efforts. **(12)** While Alan was able to advance his career, Barbara was the homemaker who took care of the children. This follows the concept of nonmonetary contributions which began with O'Brien v. O'Brien (husband's medical degree subject to equitable distribution because it was earned during marriage and wife quit job and maintained family while husband earned degree). **(13)**

Therefore, the entire amount of the account should be divided in half, giving $500,000 to each spouse. An issue arises, however, because the pension, although vested, will not begin to pay out until 2017. This issue is resolved rather easily because the amounts determined in equitable distribution do not always require liquidation of the property subject to distribution. So Alan may choose to pay $500,000 to Barbara with some other amount of money (perhaps the marital home and/or Alan's interest in the Towers). **(14)** An illustration of such can be noted by the marital home: although it is subject to equal distribution between Alan and Barbara, the court will not force a sale of the home, but allow either party to "buy" the other spouse's interest or trade the interest for some other asset.

2. The issue is whether Alan's job and the desires of David to live with his father will be considered when the court determines the custody arrangements. **(15)**

First and foremost, the best interests of the child are paramount. **(16)** While both parents are generally considered fit to have custody over the children, there is no longer the presumption that the children are better off with the mother having primary custody. **(17)**

When some children are old enough, courts will consider the child's request regarding custody. Although David has expressed an interest in living with his father, the facts suggest that David's motivation is a result of Alan's influence and bias against Barbara. The fact that Alan travels frequently with his job and would need a nanny should he get custody is a factor when determining custody, but it is not outcome dependent. Moreover, the law guardian believes that the anger David has towards his mother is temporary. **(18)**

The law guardian's observations, coupled with Alan's stated desire to only see Corrine during holidays, suggests that the court would grant the couple joint custody, giving Barbara physical custody, with an alternative arrangement to be decided to allow Alan some visitation rights. The past arrangement during the marriage suggests that this situation would be in the children's best interests and would not cause a large disruption in the current family lifestyle. Therefore, Barbara should be granted physical custody. **(19)**

3. The issue is what amount should the court award Barbara when determining child support.

Currently, New York uses a formula which factors in each parent's ability to pay (income, amount received from equitable distribution) and the number of children involved. Generally, a specific percentage is taken from the non-custodial's income up to $80,000. Any income above $80,000 is left up to the judge to decide whether to consider the additional ability to pay.

In this case, Barbara will not be required to pay child support if she is the primary physical custodian of the young children. Alan will be required to pay Barbara an amount determined by the judge. The judge will also consider the needs of the children and the current lifestyle to which they are maintaining. These are just a few of the 11 factors used in determining child support. The court should therefore order Alan to pay Barbara child support in an amount to be determined by the court. **(20)**

Your Comments

(1) _____

_____

_____

(2) _____

_____

_____

(3) _____

_____

_____

(4) _____

_____

_____

(5) _____

_____

_____

(6) _____

_____

_____

(7) _____

_____

_____

(8) _____

_____

_____

(9) _____

_____

_____

(10) _____

_____

_____

(11) _____

_____

_____

(12) _____

_____

_____

(13) _____

_____

_____

(14) _____

_____

_____

(15) _____

_____

_____

(16) _____

_____

_____

(17) _____

_____

_____

(18) _____

_____

_____

(19) _____

_____

_____

(20) _____

_____

_____

Our Analysis

(1) A more effective way to organize this would be to start with an explanation of marital property versus individual property, and how the courts divide it.

(2) Try to avoid parentheses in an essay. Because the information is part of your analysis, it should be part of the sentence structure, not treated as a side note.

(3) In an effort to distinguish between the assets of the *actual* building and the *appreciation value* of the building, the author was not clear and the statement seems contradictory. First, the author stated that since Barbara owned the property prior to the marriage, it will be nonmarital property, and then discussed how assets are distributed. This is very confusing. A better way around this, which I cannot mention enough, is to CLEARLY lay out the rule and then apply it.

(4) What is the legal term for this? The author should have discussed passive versus active appreciation here. Also, when possible, be sure to use legal terminology. This is part of laying out the applicable rule.

(5) I don't see a big difference between this sentence and the sentence prior to it. Avoid restating or redundancies. The author should have discussed *what* the joint efforts were of both parties that increased the value.

(6) The author already stated this. Remember, time is not your friend on this exam, so avoid being repetitive. I know, we are being repetitive, but we are not under time constraints!

(7) This analysis is generally confusing. Do not make things more difficult on yourself, as the bar exam is already difficult enough as it is. Clearly lay out a rule, explain the rule, and then analyze. Do not go back and forth, as it will only add to your confusion and even more important, to the confusion of the examiner. Also, the author did not discuss how the building will be divided up. Will one party buy the other party out? Will it just be divided 50/50?

(8) I have stated this before, but it is worth noting over and over again. Words like *generally, maybe,* and *perhaps* indicate that you are unsure of yourself. Do not use them. People want lawyers that are sure of themselves.

(9) Great rule, but irrelevant in this analysis. This is not a memory test—use only the rules you plan to apply.

(10) In this paragraph, for better essay flow, I would suggest the author begin first with discussing when the house was acquired instead of starting with the appreciation in value. In addition, the author mentions that the property was held as tenants in the entirety, but doesn't explain why that is relevant for the purposes of determining whether or not this will be considered martial property.

(11) Again, specifically what will happen?

(12) What are these indirect efforts? Be specific. Why is it good policy that Barbara gets half the pension?

(13) Avoid parentheses. This is important stuff—it's *why* the case is important—and should not be treated as an FYI. Also, if you mention a case, it is important to compare the facts of that case with the question. The examiners don't care that the author knows what happened in O'Brien

v. O'Brien—anyone with Internet access can know that! The author drew the conclusion that this case should follow O'Brien—what the author doesn't do is explain *why*.

(14) Be careful of word choice and be sure you say what you mean. Barbara probably would not be pleased with Alan if he tried to pay her $500,000 with "some other amount of money" (unless, of course, it's more than $500,000).

(15) Use plain English. This is not a test of how well you know your thesaurus, but a test of the law. Save the 50-cent words for Scrabble.

(16) This is not really the issue. The true issue is custody in general. The question just asks "how should the court rule with regard to custody." Do not make the issue more specific than what they ask; only answer what is being asked.

(17) Okay, so what does this mean? This is your opportunity to explain the rule. This IS a legal exam; show that you know the law.

(18) This is a great start to an analysis under bar exam conditions—while not perfect, to the reader, it is clear the author understood the rule and how he believes the court may apply the facts to the rule.

(19) There are many issues to be tackled here, and the examinee does not go nearly far enough. The bar examiners are not looking for your conclusion, but rather how you got to that conclusion. Here there is very little analysis.

(20) Based on what? Always explain yourself! The exam is testing how WELL you can explain yourself, so don't skimp on this part!

General Comments

The author did a decent job on the essay answers; however, as you can see, there are many ways the author could have improved his answer to receive additional points. Overall, the author could have strengthened the analysis throughout the essay. The author knew the rules and stated his conclusions. However, it is HOW you get from the rule to the conclusion that the examiners care about. Tying the facts of the question in with the rule of law is a necessary part of analyzing a question. Practicing writing out essays and reviewing your writing is one excellent way to strengthen your exam writing skills.

CONTRACTS/CORPORATIONS

Question 2 Revisited, Evaluated in Question 9 As Well

Ana, Bob and Cal were the sole directors and sole shareholders of Feet, Inc., a closely held New York corporation which owned and operated retail shoe stores. Ana, Bob and Cal each owned 75 shares in the company. On January 2, 2002, Ana Bob and Cal signed a written shareholders' agreement which provided in pertinent part:

> Upon the death of any shareholder, Feet, Inc. shall, within sixty (60) days of receipt of a written demand from a duly appointed estate representative, purchase the shares of the deceased shareholder for $1,000 per share.

When the agreement was signed, the three directors orally agreed that the buy back provision would apply only if the corporation was making a profit.

In addition to being a director of Feet, Inc., Ana was also a licensed real estate broker and the sole director and shareholder of Ana's Realty, Ltd., a New York corporation. In June 2007, the directors of Feet, Inc., with Ana participating, voted to enter into a contract with Ana's Realty, Ltd. Prior to the vote, Ana disclosed to Bob and Cal that she was the sole shareholder and director of Ana's Realty, Ltd. The vote was two to one with Cal voting against the contract. The written contract provided that if Ana's Realty, Ltd. located a store for Feet Inc. to purchase, Ana's Realty, Ltd. would receive the customary commission of six per cent (6%) of the sales price when title closed. Ana soon found a desirable store at a favorable price, and in October 2007, Feet, Inc. purchased it.

In November 2007, Ana sent a written purchase order to Sal, the president of Shoe Co., and ordered 2,000 pairs of boots, to be delivered to the new store on or about December 1, 2007. The terms of the purchase order called for payment in full upon delivery.

On December 1, 2007, Shoe Co. delivered 2,000 pairs of running shoes to Feet, Inc.'s new store. Ana immediately had the shoes placed in an unlocked storage shed on Feet, Inc.'s property and notified Sal that she was rejecting the shoes. Sal told Ana that the shoes would be picked up within the week. However, three days later the shoes were stolen, and Sal told Ana that he was holding Feet, Inc. responsible for the loss of the shoes.

Cal died in December 2007. On February 1, 2008, Executor was duly appointed as the executor of Cal's estate. Executor gave Ana and Bob a written demand that Feet, Inc. purchase Cal's shares of stock pursuant to the written shareholders' agreement. Bob then informed Executor that Feet Inc. had not made a profit for the past three years, and therefore, the corporation would not buy back Cal's shares. Executor has confirmed that Feet, Inc. has not made a profit for the past three years.

(a) Is Feet, Inc. liable to Shoe Co. for the loss of the running shoes?
(b) Was the contract between Feet, Inc. and Ana's Realty, Ltd. voidable?
(c) Is evidence of the oral agreement admissible in an action by Executor to enforce Feet Inc.'s obligation to purchase Cal's shares of stock under the written shareholders' agreement?

Actual Past Bar Exam Answer to Question 5

Score = 52.87

a. The issue is which laws of contract apply to the question at bar. **(1)**

Under the UCC-2, which govern the law of contracts of the sale of goods apply **(2)** and the contract is between two merchants. **(3)** Here, the goods are shoes and the contract is between the seller, Shoe Co., and buyer, Feet Co., both of whom deal in the same type of business, shoe wear. **(4)** The issue is who bears the risk of loss in the contract for the sale of goods. **(5)** Ordinarily, the risk of loss remains with the seller until the goods are identified to the contract, or the contract is a destination contract, which is indicated by the words "F.O.B, buyers/sellers place of business." Since the wording "FOB" is not explicitly stated on the contract or purchase agreement/order, the risk of loss remains with the seller until the goods are accepted/and identified to the contract, and delivered. **(6)**

It must further be noted that a contract exists because under the UCC-2, which governs the contract law for a sale of goods, the only term which is required to be put in the contract to make it enforceable is the quantity. Here, the quantity of goods is in the contract itself, which is 2,000 pairs of boots, so the contract is enforceable under the UCC-2. The UCC-2 is somewhat of a more lax requirement for the formation of a contract, which applies to the sale of goods, and does not require the formalities of a contract under common law, which requires an offer, an agreement, consideration, somewhat of a "meeting of the minds." Here, it is not the case, so the Uniform Commercial Code-2 applies to this contract, which is for the sale of goods. **(7)**

The issue is who is liable for the loss of goods when they are not accepted upon delivery. **(8)** Under the UCC-2, which governs the sale of goods **(9)** when goods that are non-conforming/not accepted by the buyer upon delivery, the seller has a right to cure w/in a reasonable time. Here it should be noted that the issue is who bears the risk of loss when items are destroyed at the buyer's place of business when the goods are not accepted by buyer. **(10)**

It should be noted that here, when deliver was made, Ana, the buyer, immediately rejected the shoes because they were nonconforming to the contract. She contacted Sal immediately and told him she was not accepting the order. At that point, the risk of loss was upon Sal, because when goods are rejected, the seller has the duty to get the goods and pick them up from the buyer's place of business. **(11)** Since Ana immediately notified Sal that she was not accepting the goods, and put them in an unlocked shed, she completed what was necessary to reject the order. **(12)**

At that point, Sal had a duty to pick up the shoes immediately, since the risk of loss remained with him, irregardless **(13)** of the fact that the shows were nonconforming. **(14)** It should be further noted that it can be argued that Ana placed the shows in an unlocked shed on Feet's Inc.'s property, but we have no further information if the property was safe or not. Since the shed was on the business's property, it is likely that there was security, and the shows were safe, and Ana was not negligent by placing the shoes in a shed where she knew that they might have been stolen. **(15)**

In conclusion, it should be noted that Sal is responsible for the loss of the shoes, since Ana complied with the rejection notification under the UCC-2, which controls the sale of goods performances and contracts. **(16)**
b. The issue is whether a contract between a corporation and a business which is owned by the director of the corporation is valid.

Under the BCL, directors of a corporation have a fiduciary duty to the corporation, a duty of loyalty, and a duty not to self-deal. **(17)** Here, Ana, a director of Feet, Inc., voted to have to corporation to enter into a contract with Ana's Realty, her own corporation. **(18)** The facts indicate that Ana did tell Bob and Cal, the two other and only other directors of Feet, Inc. that she owned Ana's Realty, Inc. **(19)**

It should be noted that a director is prohibited from self-dealing. **(20)** Here, Ana did disclose that she owned Ana's Realty, and she even voted for the corporations to do business together. It can be concluded that Ana did not breach her fiduciary duty & duty of self-dealing when she did disclose this fact. **(21)**

Further, under the BCL, it should be noted that a corporation may enter into a contract with another corporation, which is owned by an interested director when that director fully discloses to the corporation that he/she is owner of the other corporation, and that the director does not have to refrain from voting in the matter. **(22)** Since Bob and Cal were notified that Ana owned Ana's Realty, Ltd., it is permissible for Ana to vote, and Ana did not breach any duty to the corporation. **(23)** Under the BCL, even if it is found that the corporations decision turned out to be nonprofitable, or losses were incurred, the directors have the defense of the Business Judgment Rule. For example, if Cal decides that the idea of the corporation entering into business with Ana's Realty was a bad idea, and it would-up that the corporation even lost money, Ana and Bob are able to assert the Business Judgment Rule ("BJR"), which states that the directors in a corporation acted under good faith and with loyalty to the corporation, and honestly believed that the undertaking was a good idea, and beneficial to the corporation. **(24)**

It should further be noted that the agreement for Ana's Realty to obtain the 6% customary commission is permissible, because under the Real Property Laws of New York, 6% is the industry standard. **(25)**

c. The issue is whether an oral agreement made prior or contemporaneous to a contract signing, and said contract is intended to be a full and final integration of the parties manifestation to enter into such agreement, enforceable? **(26)**

d. Under the NYGOL **(27)** The Parole Evidence Rule bars any oral statements prior to or contemporaneous with a signed writing, when the signed writing is meant to be a final integration.

Here, the shareholders agreement seems to be a final integration of the parties to the agreement. When it was signed by all three members, it should have been entered into the contract that the buy-back provision would apply only if the corporation was making a profit. **(28)**

Here, when executor demanded that Ana & Bob purchase the shares back from Cal's estate, Ana & Bob were obligated to do so. The oral agreement that it would only have to buy back the shares if the corp was making a profit is an oral agreement which was barred by the Parole Evidence Rule. **(29)**

It should be noted that the only time/instance that an oral agreement may be allowed to enter into the contract terms is to define the terms of the contract, or when the contract does not seem as a final and integrated agreement. **(30)** Here, this is not the case and that it should be noted that the oral agreement is barred due to the Parole Evidence Rule, as applies to Common Law, under the NYGOL. **(31)**

Your Comments

(1) _____

_____

_____

(2) _____

_____

_____

(3) _____

_____

_____

(4) _____

_____

_____

(5) _____

_____

_____

(6) _____

_____

_____

(7) _____

_____

_____

(8) _____

_____

_____

(9) _____

_____

_____

(10) _____

_____

_____

(11) _____

_____

_____

(12) _____

_____

_____

(13) _____

_____

_____

(14) _____

_____

_____

(15) _____

_____

_____

(16) _____

_____

_____

(17) _____

_____

_____

(18) _____

_____

_____

(19) _____

_____

_____

(20) _____

_____

_____

(21) _____

_____

_____

(22) _____

_____

_____

(23) _____

_____

_____

(24) _____

_____

_____

(25) _____

_____

_____

(26) _____

_____

_____

(27) _____

_____

_____

(28) _____

_____

_____

(29) _____

_____

_____

(30) _____

_____

_____

(31) _____

_____

_____

Our Analysis

(1) This is a good starting point, but not the entire issue. You always want to at least CONSIDER this first, however, because when dealing with contracts you can never properly answer a question unless you know whether to apply UCC-2 or common law. The issue is whether Feet, Inc. bears the risk of loss when the running shoes were stolen.

(2) Be careful with grammar—the word "apply" doesn't belong.

(3) Make sure that you state the law accurately. The author seems to suggest that the UCC-2 applies *only* when there is a sale of goods between two merchants. There are simply different rules that apply when dealing with merchants, as in this example.

(4) This is awkward, which makes the point you are trying to convey harder to understand. While this is not a test of your English skills, it is helpful to convey your point in a straightforward and easy-to-follow manner.

(5) This is a good issue, but it is a bit buried. You want to make your issue statements clear.

(6) This is a good example of laying out the rule, but the rule starts to get confusing. As you can see, it's not clear what the author is trying to convey in this paragraph.

(7) This is good, albeit a bit redundant. No one is arguing that the UCC does not apply, so there is no need to go into so much detail.

(8) GOOD—but the author already stated that the issue is who bears the risk of loss, so there is no need to repeat the issue.

(9) This is repetitive. The author already stated that the UCC-2 governs the sale of goods.

(10) The issue has now been restated three times. This is odd and confusing.

(11) This is an example of a good rule and application.

(12) GOOD!

(13) This is not a word. Again, it's not an English exam, but this is no time to make up your own language!

(14) Wrong standard. The correct standard to apply is that he needs to pick up in a reasonable time.

(15) The author is assuming too much. The bar examiners are telling you that the shed is unlocked so that you know Ana was negligent in safe-keeping the property. Do not over-think facts or assume facts that are not explicitly stated, such as security.

(16) This is a wrong conclusion. All of the issues are addressed, and the rules of law are laid out. However, the author comes to a wrong conclusion, and repeats himself far too often.

(17) Good rule.

(18) Why is this important? What do we call it? The author should have used legal terminology here and referred to her as an interested director.

(19) Again, why is this important? The author needs to lay out rules first, or at least standards. Try to avoid restating facts in your answer. The examiners already know the facts—what's important is how the facts apply to the rules.

(20) This applies the incorrect standard. A director is not prohibited from entering into deals with the corporation. She just needs to follow the proper procedure. Interested directors cannot vote when the contract involves self-dealing.

(21) Is disclosure alone enough? The author contradicts himself. First, the author states a rule that a director is prohibited from self-dealing. Then, the author restates facts with no basis of how they apply to the rule. Finally, the author draws a conclusion that contradicts the rule stated. You may not remember every rule of law when you take the exam, but it is important that you keep your analysis and conclusion consistent with your rule.

(22) This is an incomplete statement of the rule. When using rules, you should strive to make them as complete as possible even if you do not know the exact language.

(23) This is again an incomplete statement of the rule.

(24) As you can see, the author raises defenses of the corporation without ever explaining why. It would have been more appropriate to lay out reasons that the transaction may be void, *then* lay out the defense to why the transaction should stand.

(25) This takes the issue off track. Here, the author gets the issue, but used the wrong rule and analysis.

(26) This is very awkward. Be sure to always write clearly.

(27) What is this? When you abbreviate things, always write it out fully the first time.

(28) This doesn't make much sense.

(29) Why? Be sure to state what you mean.

(30) This is not entirely true. Remember that contracts *can* be oral, so be careful of the language you choose.

(31) The author makes it sound like the agreement should only be barred because it is oral, which is not entirely true. It is barred because the agreement is fully integrated and there is no ambiguity. We suggest stating the rule in its entirety or deleting altogether.

WILLS AND TRUSTS *Evaluated in Question 8 As Well*

In May 2006, Ron was diagnosed with a rare disease that made him physically weak, though he remained mentally alert. Thereafter, Ron had Lawyer draft a will which included, in pertinent part, the following paragraphs:

(1) I give to my Trustee the sum of $1,000,000 to be held in separate and equal trusts for my sisters, Lynn and Ethel, with the income paid to each beneficiary annually until her death, when the principal is to be paid to the estate of the beneficiary.

(2) I give the rest, residue and remainder of my estate to my dear friend, Fred, without whose loyalty and friendship I never would have been able to achieve the success I had in my life.

(3) I nominate Fred as Executor of my estate and Trustee of the trusts created herein for my sisters.

(4) My Executor and Trustee shall not be liable for any failure on his part to exercise reasonable care, diligence and prudence in the administration of my estate or the trusts created herein.

(5) Anyone who shall contest this will for any reason whatsoever shall forfeit any right that may have accrued to him or her under the provisions of this will.

Lawyer brought the will to Ron's bedside where Ron's neighbors, Sam and Dave, were present to witness his will. Ron read the will, told Lawyer it was exactly what he wanted, and declared to Sam and Dave that it was his will and he wanted them to witness the will's execution. Lawyer gave Ron a pen with which to sign his name, but because Ron was so physically weak, he was unable to lift his arm. At Ron's request, Lawyer held Ron's arm while he signed the will at the end. Sam and Dave watched and then signed the will as witnesses.

Ron died in August 2006. He never married and had no children. At the time of his death, his net estate was worth $5 million. Lawyer filed Ron's will for probate. Ethel, a competent adult, timely filed an objection to probate claiming that the will was not properly executed.

The court denied Ethel's objection, admitted Ron's will to probate, and granted letters testamentary and letters of trusteeship to Fred. No appeal was taken.

In September 2006, Fred took control of the estate assets and funded the testamentary trust for Lynn. Fred did not fund the trust for Ethel, relying on paragraph (5) of the will. After paying all creditors, Fred paid the balance of the estate to himself as residuary beneficiary.

As trustee of the trust for Lynn, Fred made an unsecured loan of $250,000 to his friend, Eric, despite his admitted knowledge that Eric had been unable to obtain any bank or other financing because of his poor credit rating. Eric is in default on the loan, having never made a single payment.

Fred recently filed his account as executor, and Ethel and Lynn filed objections thereto, (a) Ethel seeking to compel Fred to fund Ethel's trust, and (b) Lynn seeking reimbursement from Fred for the loss of trust funds from the default of the loan to Eric. Fred does not dispute the facts of the loan transaction.

(1) Did the court properly deny Ethel's objection to probate?

(2) How should the court rule on objections (a) and (b)?

Actual Past Bar Exam Answer to Question 6

Score = 52.58

(1) The issue is whether the will was properly executed. **(1)**

Under EPTL, a will is properly executed if testator signs, at the end of the will, in the present or acknowledge signature to, at least two witnesses who also sign and to whom testator publishes the will (i.e. disclose to witnesses that it is his will). **(2)**

Here, the facts that state that Ron executed his will in the presence of two witnesses and he disclosed to them that it was his will and sign it actually in their presence and the witnesses also signed. **(3)** It is irrelevant that the lawyer helped Ron by sustaining his arm because he did so under Ron's consent and direction because Ron was too weak to do so and so it is justified under the rules of the EPTL and is not an issue. **(4)**

Thus, the court properly granted probation and denied Ethel's contest. **(5)**

To the issue that the executor is also a beneficiary it will not render the will invalid because a will doesn't fail for lack of executor, the court will name one if necessary and the gift is void unless there are clear evidence that the executor is a close family member of a long time friend of testator. Here this exception applies because the executor is a long time friend of Ron. Even if not, that wouldn't affect the validity of the will as explained the court would nominate a new one. **(6)**

The executor's legacy will also be valid absent any showing of duress, fraud or undue influence, which is not the case here. **(7)**

(2) (a) The issue is whether a non-contest clause in a will must be given full enforcement

Under EPTL, a non-contest clause in a proper executed will be generally be given full recognition and enforcement in NY because it is recognized as legitimate part of the testator's wishes and will so be respected. **(8)** Unless, the will is actually held invalid or the clause is proven to have been made under an undue duress or the result of fraud.

Here, the non-contest clause is part of a valid will and there is no exceptions available. **(9)** Even under public policy such clause is given credit to stop contestants in bad faith from bringing false claims to contest a valid will. The clause says that if a beneficiary contests should not receive her legacy. There is no evidence of any duress or fraud so the clause is valid. **(10)**

The clause specifically call for forfeiture and so the court should withhold Fred's decision to bar Ethel's legacy proper and denied Ethel's motion to compel distribution of her legacy. **(11)**

(2)(b) The issue is whether Fred breached his fiduciary duties as trustee. **(12)**

Under, EPTL a disclaim clause calling for release of a fautly trustee is generally not valid and is unenforceable. The duties of a trustee is listed under the EPTL while his liabilities is provided for in the NY Fiduciary Act that provides for all trustees, administrators and executors. **(13)**

Under the NY Fiduciaries Act, adopted in NY **(14)**, a trustee is under the absolute fiduciary duty to act with care, loyalty and good faith and cannot negligently dispose of the trust's fund and may not act in gross negligence causing beneficiary's damages. Although the court will generally not hold a trustee liable for a prudent and reasonable business decision it will hold him or her at fault if he or she acts unreasonably and negligently. **(15)**

Here, executor acted wrong because he didn't secure the loan now the beneficiary has the choice to adopt his actions or to sue for an accounting where trustee may explain his actions and she or he may sue for damages through a surcharge action to recover damages and the court will grant reimbursement of the amount of the trust funds in default. **(16)**

Here, negligence of the trustee is clear for he didn't sucure the loan. **(17)** Also, he will be personally liable for the damages and a reasonable and prudent trustee always purchase liability insurance. So, if he has not done so, he will still be liable for the amount entered in favor of the aggrieved beneficiary.

Your Comments

(1) _____

_____

_____

(2) _____

_____

_____

(3) _____

_____

_____

(4) _____

_____

_____

(5) _____

_____

_____

(6) _____

_____

_____

(7) _____

_____

_____

(8) _____

_____

_____

(9) _____

_____

_____

(10) _____

_____

_____

(11) _____

_____

_____

(12) _____

_____

_____

(13) _____

_____

_____

(14) _____

_____

_____

(15) _____

_____

_____

(16) _____

_____

_____

(17) _____

_____

_____

Our Analysis

(1) While accurate, this issue can be expanded to say "… executed when a testator has assistance from his attorney to sign the will.…"

(2) This is technically a good statement of the rule, but does not state all requirements and is not very eloquent.

(3) The author simply restated facts in this sentence. Your analysis should compare the facts to the rule. This might be as simple as adding a few words, such as "when" and "because."

(4) The author states that it is irrelevant that the lawyer held the testator's arm. But it is not irrelevant, as it is a main issue. Does it matter that the lawyer held his arm? What is the rule on this? State the rule, that it's okay for another to effectuate the signature, so long as the testator is directing and viewing the signature, then say, "because here testator ..." and apply the facts.

(5) This conclusion should be at the end of the question. It's an odd transition to conclude and then go on to state more.

(6) Yet again, this paragraph is just confusing. State a clear rule—where is the rule on executorship? THEN bring in the facts. The first part of this question has very few well-articulated rules, and even though it hits on the issues and brings in facts, it would do better with a clear picture of the rules.

(7) Why? The analysis is always the most important part of the essay, so NEVER leave it out. EVER.

(8) This is a better rule statement.

(9) Lay out the exceptions in the rule. Just saying "there are exceptions" is too vague. This is your analysis section, probably the most important part of the essay. You need to analyze why there are no exceptions.

(10) What is the argument that there is no duress or fraud? Ethel is arguing that there is duress because the attorney helped the testator sign the will. As the author, you want to be clear why she will probably not win that argument. Remember that the bar examiners want to know if you will be a good lawyer, and part of that is putting forth an ARGUMENT, and being persuasive.

(11) This just goes from rule to conclusion, with no analysis.

(12) The issue is actually whether Lynn can be reimbursed by Fred for the loss of trust funds, not whether Fred breached his fiduciary duty as trustee. While that is going to be a factor in your analysis, you want to be sure that you understand the issue of the question.

(13) This statement does not make sense. We assume it is supposed to be a rule, but it is not very clear. We have stated this many times, but it is imperative that a rule be very clear.

(14) Avoid redundancies. If it's the NY Fiduciaries Act, it's adopted in NY.

(15) This is a better rule paragraph.

(16) There is no analysis in this paragraph. Why is the trustee negligent for failing to secure the loan? Does the executor have any argument that he is not negligent? Address this before moving into the beneficiary's options.

(17) Again, the author hasn't said why. We have said it numerous times, but the examiners are testing your abilities to analyze, so ALWAYS tell them why.

General Comments

Compare with Question 8, which received a lower score.

General Comments on Essays That Receive Scores in the 50s
Most of these essays are getting the right issues. However, they are not laying out the rules as well as those essays that received scores in the 60s. They are also significantly lacking in the analysis, which, as we have said ad nauseam, is absolutely the most important thing you need to have. Scores in the 50s can still be passing (although not always), but you want to aim higher, and to get that higher score you need to ALWAYS lay out rules clearly and ALWAYS explain the "why."

CRIMINAL LAW

When Joe refused to pay a gambling debt he owed to Mark, Mark told Joe that he knew members of a gang and that he would have them kill Joe. Both Mark and Joe are adults. Mark then contacted Ron and Sam, both age 15 and members of a local gang. Mark asked them to give Joe a severe beating but expressly told them not to use weapons.

Two days later, while looking for Joe, Ron and Sam, who were unarmed, saw him getting into his car in a parking lot. They began to run toward Joe. Joe saw them running toward him and noticed they were wearing bandanas indicative of gang membership. Thinking that Mark had sent them to kill him, Joe reached in the glove compartment of his car for a handgun and shot at Ron and Sam, wounding both. Although Joe explained Mark's threat to the police, he was arrested and charged with two counts of assault in the first degree. Ron and Sam were also arrested and charged with attempted assault. Based on Joe's explanation and statements given to the police by Ron and Sam, Mark was arrested and charged with conspiracy and criminal solicitation.

Based on the foregoing facts:
(a) If Joe raises the defense of justification, is it likely to be successful?
(b)(1) Did the actions of Ron and Sam constitute the crime of attempt to commit an assault?
    (2) If so, do Ron and Sam have any defenses?
(c) Did Mark commit the crimes of
    (1) conspiracy and
    (2) criminal solicitation?

Actual Past Bar Exam Answer to Question 7

Score = 48.8

a. The issue here is what type of defense is justification and what are the elements of the defense of justification. **(1)**

b. Under the New York Penal Law, the defense of justification is an affirmative defense and must be raised by the defendant and must be proven by a fair preponderance of the evidence. **(2)**

Here, the issue if whether or not Mark was justified in shooting Ron and Sam, and wounding both. **(3)**

The facts indicate that Mark **(4)** was charged with two counts of assault in the first degree. Under NYPL, assault in the first degree constitutes assault, which is intended to instilling a fear of immediate battery in an individual, coupled with the use of a firearm, or displaying a firearm, in which serious injury or death occurs. **(5)**

Under the NYPL, justification is an affirmative defense to the crime of assault, which is a criminal battery. **(6)**

It can be argued by Joe that he was in fear for his life, because he has threatened by Mark,**(7)** who had told him that he knew members of a gang and that he would have them kill Joe. Further, it may be argued that when, 2 days later, Joe saw Ron and Sam, who were unarmed, running toward him with bandanas, indicative of gang membership, Joe has justified in protecting himself because he was warned by Mark that this may happen. Just because Ron and Sam were wearing bandanas had no bearing on the fact that they were gang members, and Joe had no reason to know that. **(8)**

Under NYPL, justification is an affirmative defense when a defendant is justified for his criminal acts. Here, even though Joe was warned by Mark **(9)** that he would have gang members come after him and kill him, his defense of justification in shooting both Ron and Sam are not justified. **(10)** Here, Mark's threat of harm was not immediate, he just said that he knew members of a gang. It was purely a threat. **(11)** It is not reasonable, after two days had lapsed, for Joe to think that Mark would have members of a local gang kill him. **(12)** The only evidence that Joe had to even think that he was going to be killed by gang members, and that he was being followed, was the fact that Sam and Ron were wearing bandanas. This fact alone, that two men were wearing bandanas, is not enough to satisfy the element for justification. **(13)**

In addition, it should be noted that the issue of self-defense, another affirmative defense of justification, is not viable. **(14)**

Under NYPL, the defense of self-defense **(15)** is an affirmative defense **(16)** and one may not use more force than reasonable and given to him. Here, Joe, when he saw both Ron and Sam, he had a duty to retreat, meaning that he was not justified in pulling out a gun from his car and shooting Ron and Sam. **(17)**

Under NYPL, a person has a duty to retreat before using deadly force, except when a person is in his/her home. "A person's home is his castle," and the duty to retreat is not necessary. **(18)** Here, since Joe was already in his car, he had a duty to retreat and just drive away, instead of reaching into his glove compartment and shooting Ron and Sam.

Thus, Joe had a duty to retreat, and the defense of self-defense, or justification, does not apply.

c.1. The issue is what are the elements of attempt? **(19)**

Under the NYPL, attempt is defined as the intent to commit a crime, and there must be an overt act in furtherance of the intended crime to constitute attempt. A guilty mind is not enough.

Under the NYPL, an assault is defined as an intended criminal battery. **(20)**

In this case, Ron and Sam's actions did not constitute the crime of attempt to commit an assault. **(21)**

As per the NYPL, to be convicted of the crime of attempt to commit an assault, a person must possess the requisite intent to commit the crime, as well as the attempt, which means an overt act in furtherance of the crime. **(22)**

Here, Ron and Sam's actions did not constitute attempt. **(23)** The facts state that they were merely running to Joe's car. The facts do not state whether or not they were intended to harm Joe. For all Joe knew, they could have been running towards Joe to tell him that he is in danger. It is purely speculative and prejudicial to assume that since both Ron and Sam were wearing bandanas and running to Joe's car, they were going to harm/beat/kill him. **(24)**

Thus, under NYPL, Sam and Ron did not posses the requisite intent for the crime of attempt.

2. The issue is what, if any, are the defenses to the crime of attempt to commit an assault? **(25)**

Under the NYPL, it should be noted that minors have a defense to a crime because they are underage. They will be penalized, but not tried as an adult. **(26)**

Further, both Sam and Joe did not do any further acts in furtherance of a possible assault on Joe. **(27)**

d.1. The issue is what are the elements of conspiracy? **(28)**

Under the NYPL, conspiracy is defined as undertaking a criminal activity with 2 or more people with the intent to carry out that crime. **(29)**

Here, it can be shown that Mark can't be held liable for conspiracy. To be liable for conspiracy, Mark must have done something more than just ask someone to beat up someone else. **(30)** Mark did not assisting in the search for Joe, Mark did not provide weapons to Ron and Sam, he did not give them any more information, or did nothing more than just ask Ron and Sam to beat up Joe.

Thus, since Mark did not aid in the commission of the assault, did not provide weapons, items to facilitate the crime, drive a getaway car, or perform any other overt acts in furtherance of the crime, Mark cannot be held liable/guilty for the crime of conspiracy, under NYPL. **(31)**

2. The issue is what are the elements of solicitation?

Under the NYPL, the elements of solicitation are inquiring or asking someone to carry out a crime.

Here, the facts show that Mark asked Ron and Sam to give Joe a severe beating, but told them not to use weapons.

Under the NYPL, Mark is guilty of solicitation to commit the crime of assault because he asked Sam and Ron to give Joe a beating.

It should be further noted that it does not matter that he told them not to use weapons. It means, under the NYPL, that Mark would be guilty of solicitation in the 3rd degree, because no weapons were involved.

Comparison Notes

Some students may at this time choose to flip back to Answer 6, which received a 52.58, and compare that answer to the answer presented to the same fact pattern above.

Note to yourself the major difference between the answer in Question 6 and the answer given here. Take a few moments to jot down your thoughts and key differences here:

Answer 6	Answer 8
(1)	(1)
(2)	(2)
(3)	(3)
(4)	(4)

Answer 6	Answer 8
(5) _____	(5) _____
_____	_____
_____	_____
(6) _____	(6) _____
_____	_____
_____	_____

Our Analysis

(1) Make sure you clearly state the issue. The elements of self-defense are not the issue, so leave this out, since the examiners want you to answer ONLY what is being asked.

(2) Good rule statement.

(3) Be sure you are using the proper names. It was Joe who shot Ron and Sam, not Mark. You do not want the bar examiners to think you are easily confused on something like names. (After all, no one wants to hire an attorney who can't even remember his client's name!) This is also where an outline might come in handy, so you do NOT become confused by something as simple as names. Come on, it is hard enough to earn points—don't lose them by getting names wrong.

(4) Actually, Joe. (Again, you have to remember your client's name, and the names of the other parties involved!)

(5) This seems a bit off course. Why is this relevant? Remember, you have VERY limited time, so make sure every sentence plays an important role in your essay.

(6) It is unclear why the author states this sentence here. Outlining an essay will help you avoid these pitfalls. The author would have avoided being redundant by restating that justification is an affirmative defense if he had included this in his rule paragraph (paragraph 2 above).

(7) This is confusing. The author seems to skip a few steps by immediately discussing that Joe was in fear of his life, alluding that Joe may have the defense of self, without first discussing what crime Joe may be charged with.

(8) This doesn't make much sense. The author says that Joe was justified, but does not really explain why. Also, the bandanas are relevant as to why they put Joe in fear and whether they would put a reasonable person in fear. The author uses the passive voice ("he was warned by Mark," "he has [was] threatened by Mark"), which makes the sentence more confusing than it needs to be. The active voice ("Mark threatened Joe," "Mark warned Joe") would have made the sentence clearer. Think of it this way, when are lawyers ever passive??!!

(9) Actually, Mark warned Joe. We know, broken record, but little things like this make the bar examiners think that you do not pay attention to detail.

(10) This sounds like the author is talking in circles. The author has now stated three times that under NYPL, justification is an affirmative defense. As an examinee, you need to lay out the rule, and then very clearly apply the facts to that rule. Do not go in circles or get caught up in irrelevant details. There seem to be a lot of conclusions without proper analysis.

(11) But we are not looking at Mark's threat, we are looking at whether the gang members were a threat. The author fails to tie together why Mark's threat is relevant in Joe's argument that Sam and Ron were a threat.

(12) Why not? Two days isn't that much time.

(13) Why not? What would a reasonable person think? This goes into your analysis. The bar examiners want to know what YOU think.

(14) Self-defense is the issue being addressed here. Because of that, this is redundant and somewhat confusing.

(15) Be careful with sentence structure: "defense of self-defense" is a redundancy.

(16) This is the fourth time the author stated this. You simply do NOT have the time.

(17) Need more explanation of a duty to retreat. Lay out the rule, but also explain the rules where necessary.

(18) Lay out the rule before analyzing. The organization here is a bit confusing and irrelevant. Since Joe was not attacked in his home, this exception does not apply. Avoid stating rules if they are irrelevant—the examiners don't care if you know rules that are inapplicable.

(19) This is not the correct issue. At any time, a law student can lay out the elements of attempt. In general, the issue will be whether the particular facts of the question meet all of the required elements of a claim or crime. If you use IRAC, be sure that you clearly state the issue presented in the fact pattern.

(20) While accurate, the author probably could have just stated the rule for an attempted assault rather than splitting it.

(21) This particular author might want to save the conclusion for the end, as the analysis is really the important part.

(22) Try not to be wordy. Here, "the crime of attempt to commit an assault" could have easily and accurately been worded as "attempted assault." As stated many times, the key is to be succinct.

(23) Again, the author isn't fully analyzing his conclusions. This disrupts the flow and may make the examiner conclude that you have not analyzed the issue properly.

(24) The author assumed too many facts and gave Sam and Ron too much of the benefit of the doubt. Do not read too much into facts. Take them at face value and apply them.

(25) The issue is not what the defenses to the crime of attempt are, but whether Ron and Sam, who are minors, have a defense against the crime of attempted assault. One way (but not the only way) to start an issue sentence is with "The issue is whether…" Your issue statement should mirror the question being asked.

(26) The author is missing the analysis of this question. The author states an NY rule, but never applies the rule to the facts. Be sure to apply all the rules that you state; the examiner isn't going to give you points if she has to fill in the blanks for you. "Oh, I bet he meant that Sam or Joe has a defense because they are minors" is not something that an examiner will award points for.

(27) There is not enough here. The author went back to the elements of assault, but did not discuss the infancy defense in enough detail. Why is this relevant?

(28) Not the issue exactly. A better issue statement would have been more specific, such as "did Mark commit the crime of conspiracy."

(29) State the rule with more specificity. In NY, a requirement is also that one of the conspirators commits an overt act in furtherance of the conspiracy.

(30) Remember to always lay out the full rule. Here the author is trying to apply a fact to part of an element of the rule that he did not define.

(31) This is the incorrect rule and there is not nearly enough application. The rule requires *one* of the conspirators to commit an overt act. Even though Mark did not commit an overt act, Mark asked Ron and Sam to beat up Joe, and Ron and Sam committed an overt act when they ran toward Joe intending to harm him.

General Comments

In general, the essay often misses a clear analysis. Sometimes the author spends too much time on facts or rules of law that are unimportant and then by the time the author gets to the end, there is not nearly enough time spent on analyzing the important issues. This is the benefit of an outline, or at the very least, thinking about what you want to write before putting pen to paper. Also, be sure to spend an equal amount of time on all parts of the question. The questions are of equal importance, so a great analysis to one sub-question followed by a poor analysis to another sub-question will hurt your points on the essay as a whole.

WILLS AND TRUSTS *Question 6 Revisited*

In May 2006, Ron was diagnosed with a rare disease that made him physically weak, though he remained mentally alert. Thereafter, Ron had Lawyer draft a will which included, in pertinent part, the following paragraphs:

> (1) I give to my Trustee the sum of $1,000,000 to be held in separate and equal trusts for my sisters, Lynn and Ethel, with the income paid to each beneficiary annually until her death, when the principal is to be paid to the estate of the beneficiary.
>
> (2) I give the rest, residue and remainder of my estate to my dear friend, Fred, without whose loyalty and friendship I never would have been able to achieve the success I had in my life.
>
> (3) I nominate Fred as Executor of my estate and Trustee of the trusts created herein for my sisters.
>
> (4) My Executor and Trustee shall not be liable for any failure on his part to exercise reasonable care, diligence and prudence in the administration of my estate or the trusts created herein.
>
> (5) Anyone who shall contest this will for any reason whatsoever shall forfeit any right that may have accrued to him or her under the provisions of this will.

Lawyer brought the will to Ron's bedside where Ron's neighbors, Sam and Dave, were present to witness his will. Ron read the will, told Lawyer it was exactly what he wanted, and declared to Sam and Dave that it was his will and he wanted them to witness the will's execution. Lawyer gave Ron a pen with which to sign his name, but because Ron was so physically weak, he was unable to lift his arm. At Ron's request, Lawyer held Ron's arm while he signed the will at the end. Sam and Dave watched and then signed the will as witnesses.

Ron died in August 2006. He never married and had no children. At the time of his death, his net estate was worth $5 million. Lawyer filed Ron's will for probate. Ethel, a competent adult, timely filed an objection to probate claiming that the will was not properly executed.

The court denied Ethel's objection, admitted Ron's will to probate, and granted letters testamentary and letters of trusteeship to Fred. No appeal was taken.

In September 2006, Fred took control of the estate assets and funded the testamentary trust for Lynn. Fred did not fund the trust for Ethel, relying on paragraph (5) of the will. After paying all creditors, Fred paid the balance of the estate to himself as residuary beneficiary.

As trustee of the trust for Lynn, Fred made an unsecured loan of $250,000 to his friend, Eric, despite his admitted knowledge that Eric had been unable to obtain any bank or other financing because of his poor credit rating. Eric is in default on the loan, having never made a single payment.

Fred recently filed his account as executor, and Ethel and Lynn filed objections thereto, (a) Ethel seeking to compel Fred to fund Ethel's trust, and (b) Lynn seeking reimbursement from Fred for the loss of trust funds from the default of the loan to Eric. Fred does not dispute the facts of the loan transaction.

(1) Did the court properly deny Ethel's objection to probate?
(2) How should the court rule on objections (a) and (b)?

Actual Past Bar Exam Answer to Question 8

Score = 47.83

1. The court properly denied Ethel's objection to probate.

The issue is whether Ethel has standing to object to the will being admitted to probate. A person has standing to contest the will when he/she would otherwise be a beneficiary eligible to take under intestacy.

Since Ron, the testator has no children or wife, his next of kin are the testator's parents. The facts do not indicate that Ron has living parents. Therefore, the next relative to inherit would be Ron's sisters, Ethel and Lynn.

Because Ethel is one of the only two people who can inherit under intestacy, she is deemed to have standing to object to probate. **(1)**

The issue is whether Ron's will was properly executed. For a will to be properly executed, it must be signed by the testator (who is with sound mind and not under any undue influence) in the presence of at least two competent, un-interested witnesses. The will must also be signed by the two witnesses, along with their names and addresses printed. Further, the testator must affirm that the contents of the will are indeed his intentions and that he intends the document to be his last will. **(2)**

In this case, Ethel's objection to the execution of the will most likely related to the testator's signature. The rule regarding the testator's signature is a broadly defined requirement. The testator need not actually sign the will himself. He can direct someone to sign his name for him. The testator can also be aided in writing his signature. For the signature to be valid, the testator must affirm before the witnesses that he intends the signature to be his. Usually, the person aiding the testator will sign his name below the testator's. **(3)**

In this case, all the facts given conform to the will formality requirements. Therefore, the court properly denied Ethel's objection. **(4)**

2. Objection (a)

The issue is whether Ethel can compel Fred to fund her trust, despite Ethel's content of the will. **(5)**

Will provisions that disqualify a beneficiary from taking under the will should the beneficiary contest the will are generally **(6)** held to be valid. Since Ethel did contest the will, she will be deemed to have forfeited her right to take under Ron's will. Therefore, Ethel cannot compel Fred to fund her trust because the gift to Ethel has adeemed (A gift is considered adeemed when the beneficiary, for some reason, cannot take the gift.) **(7)**

Alternatively, Ethel may have an argument that she did not actually contest the will itself, but merely the proper execution of such. Should the court agree with Ethel, she may then compel Fred to fund her trust and pay her income of the trust during her lifetime. **(8)**

Objection (b)

The issue is whether a trustee can be held liable for breach of his fiduciary duties when a will provision attempts to relieve the trustee from any such duties.

While a person is free to grant and restrict the trustee and executor with powers as the testator sees fit, one cannot relieve a trustee from his basic fiduciary duties to both the will beneficiaries and the testator. **(9)**

Because Fred is subject to take the remainder and residuary of Ron's estate, he has an interest that conflicts with his duties as trustee and executor. Although Fred has what seems to be free reign over the estate, clause (4) does not relieve Fred of the obligations of clause (1). Therefore, Fred would be in breach of his fiduciary duties to Lynn by recklessly managing the trust set up in clause (1). **(10)**

A fiduciary has a general obligation to not engage in self-dealing. **(11)** Fred's loan to his friend Eric, despite Fred's knowledge of Eric's poor credit, is considered self-dealing. Fred could have loaned Eric money from the residuary estate that Fred was entitled to. Instead, Fred used funds from Lynn's trust. This is a form of self-dealing because Fred sough to relieve himself from any monetary loss by using money that belonged to someone else, knowing full well that Eric was a big risk. **(12)**

Fred breached his duty and clause (4) does not relieve Fred of his liability to Lynn. **(13)** Therefore, Lynn can properly seek reimbursement from Fred as a result of the loss of money in Lynn's trust due to Fred's risky loan to Eric. A beneficiary of a will may properly sue the trustee and/or executor for breaching any or all of the fiduciary duties. **(14)**

Lastly, should the court strictly construe clause (4), it would be against public policy to do so. Not allowing Lynn to recover would give all future trustees and administrators little incentive to exercise due care in managing the estate. Courts will not allow such a thing to take place. If they did, trustees in positions like Fred's could pretty much take all the money for themselves without any threat of consequences.

It is therefore also equitable for Lynn to be able to recover from Fred.

Your Comments

(1) _____

_____

_____

(2) _____

_____

_____

(3) _____

_____

_____

(4) _____

_____

_____

(5) _____

_____

_____

(6) _____

_____

_____

(7) _____

_____

_____

(8) _____

_____

_____

(9) _____

_____

_____

(10) _____

_____

_____

(11) _____

_____

_____

(12) _____

_____

_____

(13) _____

_____

_____

(14) _____

_____

_____

Our Analysis

(1) This is all good. However, the issue was not really whether Ethel had standing, but whether the will was properly executed. The question asks whether the court properly denied her request, which should alert you to the fact that the question is REALLY asking, "Is this a valid will?"

(2) Good. You do want to lay out the issue first, then the rule, and any explanation of the rule. However, to make the rule even clearer, it is a good idea to number or letter the parts of the rule. For instance "For a rule to be properly executed, it must be a) signed by the testator...."

(3) To strengthen your analysis, instead of naming the generic party of the rule, i.e., any "testator," name the party identified in the facts, i.e., "*Ron*" (the testator in these facts) that the rule should be applied to.

For example, stating *"Ron* need not actually sign the will himself.... *Ron* can also be aided in writing his signature ..." is easy to do and makes the analysis much clearer. Making that minor edit will change a paragraph from being simply the rule (applied to *any* "testator" and not necessarily the testator of these facts) to an analysis of these facts to that rule (the rule applied to *this* testator).

(4) The author did not analyze the issue but simply restated the rules and with a conclusion. The author properly focused on the testator's signature being the issue, but does not even confirm that the other requirements of a valid will are met. Even a brief statement in passing would suffice.

(5) The author probably meant "contest" and not "content." It is important to pay attention to your spelling and typos on a bar exam.

(6) Are they or are they not in New York? Using words like *generally* indicates to the bar examiner that you are unsure. You don't want the bar examiner to think you don't know the law AND you don't know where you are! Know the law in NY and apply it appropriately. Also, use the legal terms if possible. What the author is referring to is a "no contest clause" and the issue is whether they are valid in NY. They are, with four exceptions.

(7) This last statement is important. It should not be included in parentheses after the analysis, but rather should appear as a sentence in the rule section.

(8) This is an incorrect application of the law. The law is that no contest clauses in NY will be upheld as valid, with four exceptions. A high scoring essay would have clearly stated this rule and then stated the four exceptions: (1) the contestant is alleging fraud or that the will was revoked by another writing; (2) the contest is on behalf of a minor or incompetent; (3) the contestant is alleging incorrect jurisdiction; or (4) the contestant is asking the court to interpret a provision, not contesting the will itself. After stating the rule, a high scoring essay would apply the four exceptions to the facts of the essay and, based on the analysis, come to the conclusion that Ethel's contest did not fit into any exception and therefore she would not take under the will.

(9) This is a good start to an NY essay. The author chose IRAC as the essay structure. The issue and rule are both clear, easy-to-read sentences stated in plain English.

(10) This seems very conclusory. A good essay states the rule, and explains the rule, before delving into any analysis. In addition, instead of stating "clause 1, clause 4," etc., state what the clauses say—the examiner isn't going to want to have to go back to the question to try to figure out what you want to say!

(11) This appears to be explaining the rule and should really be first and foremost in the essay.

(12) While not perfect, this is a good analysis of how self-dealing may apply to this fact pattern.

(13) Why not? There is no explanation of any rule on point, or how NY interprets such a rule. Be wary of being conclusory. A good essay clearly lays out rules and applies them.

(14) Again, this sentence is a rule and doesn't belong in this paragraph.

General Comments

Overall, when you chose an essay structure, be sure that you follow it. Here the author seemed to use an IRAC essay structure, but did not properly follow the structure. The author included rules in incorrect places. In addition, the author could strengthen his essay analysis of the rules. Remember, the analysis is the most important part of your essay.

CONTRACTS/CORPORATIONS

Questions 2 and 5 Revisited

Ana, Bob and Cal were the sole directors and sole shareholders of Feet, Inc., a closely held New York corporation which owned and operated retail shoe stores. Ana, Bob, and Cal each owned 75 shares in the company. On January 2, 2002, Ana, Bob and Cal signed a written shareholders' agreement which provided in pertinent part:

> Upon the death of any shareholder, Feet, Inc. shall, within sixty (60) days of receipt of a written demand from a duly appointed estate representative, purchase the shares of the deceased shareholder for $1,000 per share.

When the agreement was signed, the three directors orally agreed that the buy back provision would apply only if the corporation was making a profit.

In addition to being a director of Feet, Inc., Ana was also a licensed real estate broker and the sole director and shareholder of Ana's Realty, Ltd., a New York corporation. In June 2007, the directors of Feet, Inc., with Ana participating, voted to enter into a contract with Ana's Realty, Ltd. Prior to the vote, Ana disclosed to Bob and Cal that she was the sole shareholder and director of Ana's Realty, Ltd. The vote was two to one with Cal voting against the contract. The written contract provided that if Ana's Realty, Ltd. located a store for Feet Inc. to purchase, Ana's Realty, Ltd. would receive the customary commission of six per cent (6%) of the sales price when title closed. Ana soon found a desirable store at a favorable price, and in October 2007, Feet, Inc. purchased it.

In November 2007, Ana sent a written purchase order to Sal, the president of Shoe Co., and ordered 2,000 pairs of boots, to be delivered to the new store on or about December 1, 2007. The terms of the purchase order called for payment in full upon delivery.

On December 1, 2007, Shoe Co. delivered 2,000 pairs of running shoes to Feet, Inc.'s new store. Ana immediately had the shoes placed in an unlocked storage shed on Feet, Inc.'s property and notified Sal that she was rejecting the shoes. Sal told Ana that the shoes would be picked up within the week. However, three days later the shoes were stolen, and Sal told Ana that he was holding Feet, Inc. responsible for the loss of the shoes.

Cal died in December 2007. On February 1, 2008, Executor was duly appointed as the executor of Cal's estate. Executor gave Ana and Bob a written demand that Feet, Inc. purchase Cal's shares of stock pursuant to the written shareholders' agreement. Bob then informed Executor that Feet Inc. had not made a profit for the past three years, and therefore, the corporation would not buy back Cal's shares. Executor has confirmed that Feet, Inc. has not made a profit for the past three years.

(a) Is Feet, Inc. liable to Shoe Co. for the loss of the running shoes?
(b) Was the contract between Feet, Inc. and Ana's Realty, Ltd. voidable?
(c) Is evidence of the oral agreement admissible in an action by Executor to enforce Feet Inc.'s obligation to purchase Cal's shares of stock under the written shareholders' agreement?

Actual Past Bar Exam Answer to Question 9

Score = 46.87

a. The issue is who bears the loss of the nonconforming goods. Feet and Shoe Co are both merchants and they entered into a valid contract for the sale of goods worth more than $500, so the Uniform Commercial Code (U.C.C) applies here. **(1)** The sales contract is valid because both merchants had the intent to enter into a contract and the quantity was in the terms. As between merchants, which Shoe Co. and Feet Inc are because they both deal in the sale of goods, the lack of price terms will not void the contract and a court will decide a reasonable price if the parties cannot agree. **(2)**

The U.C.C. provides that the risk of loss of goods remain with the seller until delivery is accepted by the buyer or the goods reach the destination provided for in the contract. Also, it is presumed that a seller will use a common carrier or other appropriate means to ensure delivery to the buyer. In such a situation, the seller is usually in a position to insure the goods with the carrier until the goods are delivered to the buyer. This puts seller in a better position to bear the risk of loss due to the availability of insurance, an option buyer does not have. **(3)**

In this case, Ana of Feet Inc accepted the nonconforming goods by taking physical possession. One a person accepts delivery, the risk of loss shifts to them. Because Ana accepted the goods, Feet Inc now bears the risk of loss for the goods.

It should be noted, however, than Ana promptly advised the seller that she was rejecting the goods due to their nonconformity. **(4)** This rejection serves to keep Foot Co liable for the nonconforming goods. Even though Shoe Co does not have possession or control of the goods, Foot Co. is liable because Ana notified Foot Co. within a reasonable time.

The issue is whether Feet Inc is liable for the shoes that were stolen while in its possession. **(5)**

An owner of property has a duty of care as a bailee for personal property that is stored there. In this case, Feet Inc's possession of the shoes was meant to be temporary because Shoe Co. stated that it would come get the rejected shoes within one week. In a bailment situation, a bailee is liable for bailed goods where he is grossly negligent. Absent gross negligence on the part of Feet Inc (which an unlocked storage shed is presumed not to be grossly negligent care), Shoe Co. is liable for the running shoes. **(6)**

b. The issue is whether a contract involving an interested party is voidable. A contract is voidable where one party's intent is adverse to the other party's. **(7)** With voidable contracts, the party who is in a position to cancel the contract may ratify the voidable contract and the contract will then be fully enforceable. Ana, as sole shareholder of Ana's Realty, Ltd, fully disclosed here interests to Bob and Cal, her fellow shareholders in Feet, Inc. Feet's Inc.'s directors/shareholders (it is a close corporation) must vote to ratify the contract and for corporations formed after February 22, 1998, a majority vote by the directors is required to allow the corporation to enter into a contract with an interested director. Because Bob and Ana voted for the contract, it was 2 votes to 1 with Cal being the dissenting director, and the contract is valid and not voidable. **(8)**

It should be noted that Cal has options available to him as a dissenting voter which he may enforce at his option.

c. The issue is whether parol evidence is admissible where there is already a written shareholder's agreement. The parol evidence rule excludes evidence from being admitted where a written contract already exists. **(9)** The only exception to this rule is where the evidence at issue explains and completes incomplete terms of the contract. **(10)**

In this case, the oral agreement was done contemporaneously with the execution of the shareholder's agreement and all of the parties expressed intent that there oral agreement be part of the written one. Because the oral agreement further explains the written agreement and does not contradict any of the written agreement's terms, the oral agreement will be admissible in an action by Cal's executor. **(11)**

Comparison Notes

Some students may at this time choose to flip back to Answer 2, which received a 60.96, and 5, which received a 53.87, and compare those answers to the answer presented to the same fact pattern above.

Note to yourself the major difference between the answer in Questions 6 and the answer given here. Take a few moments to jot down your thoughts and key differences here:

Answer 2	Answer 5	Answer 9
(1)	(1)	(1)
(2)	(2)	(2)
(3)	(3)	(3)
(4)	(4)	(4)
(5)	(5)	(5)
(6)	(6)	(6)

Our Analysis

(1) Be careful here. The author makes it sound like the UCC only applies to the sale of goods over $500, when in reality it applies to all goods. The author confused the UCC-2 application to the sale of goods with the requirement that a contract for sale of goods over $500 needs to be in writing to satisfy the Statute of Frauds.

(2) Good section for the most part, BUT, how do we know the merchants had the intent? Use the facts. You have to.

(3) Good explanation of the rule, but it is not all relevant to the facts. The bar examiners want you to fully explain the rule, but only so much as is relevant. Why is insurance relevant here? Sure, it might explain WHY the seller bears the risk, but it is also going into too much theory. Just explain the rule. Also, this misses the issue since the running shoes were stolen after delivery and risk of loss usually applies to loss or damage while in transit.

(4) Is Ana rejecting them or accepting them? This contradicts the above paragraph. Avoid telling the bar examiner one thing, and then changing your mind. No one wants a wishy washy advocate!

(5) This is the real issue, which makes the bar examiner think you just wasted her time by writing the above paragraph.

(6) Why is there negligence? What constitutes gross negligence? You have to bring in the facts to get a high score on any essay.

(7) First, this rule is too general. You have to be very specific when stating rules. Second, and perhaps it is because this rule is too broad, it is simply not true. Just because one party's interest is adverse does not make a contract voidable. This rule needs to be stated in a more specific way, with respect to corporations.

(8) Here, the law is incorrect. Ana, the interested party, should not have her vote counted.

(9) All types of evidence? Again, this is too broad, and doesn't clearly state the rule for parol evidence.

(10) This is not the only exception, nor is it an accurate statement of law.

(11) Be careful with your law application. The author has the correct rule but applies it incorrectly. Here, the oral agreement does not *explain* the written agreement because the agreement is clear on its face. The oral agreement is actually an additional term that was not incorporated into the written agreement.

WILLS

Theresa, a widower, asked her close friend, Ann, an attorney, to draft a Will for her and to serve as the Executrix of Theresa's estate. Ann orally advised Theresa that she could draft the Will and that anyone could serve as an Executrix, even a lay person. Ann also stated that as Executrix, she would be entitled to commissions, and as an attorney, she also would be entitled to receive legal fees for the administration of Theresa's estate. Theresa told Ann that she wanted to leave her diamond ring and her Picasso painting to her only child, Debra; the sum of $200,000 to Ann, in consideration of their close friendship; and the balance of her estate to Debra's daughter, Gina.

In December 2003, Theresa went to Ann's office to sign the Will that Ann had drafted. After reviewing the document, ensuring that it accurately reflected her intent, and declaring it her Will, Theresa signed the Will in front of Debra and Ann's secretary, Jane. Both signed as witnesses, and each signed an affidavit attesting to the execution of the Will.

The Will contained the following provisions:

(1) I give my diamond ring and my Picasso painting to my daughter, Debra;
(2) I give $200,000 to my attorney and friend, Ann, in consideration of our close, long-term friendship;
(3) I leave the residue of my estate to my granddaughter, Gina;
(4) I appoint my attorney, Ann, as Executrix.

In February 2007, Theresa sold the Picasso painting to a private collector for $3 million dollars. She immediately opened a new account in her name only at Big Bank and deposited the proceeds into that account. Theresa died on December 15, 2007, survived by Ann, Debra and Gina. Theresa left a net estate of $5 million dollars, consisting of her home, various stocks and bonds, the bank account in her name in Big Bank, containing only the proceeds of the sale of the Picasso painting, and her diamond ring, valued at $50,000.

Thereafter, Ann filed Theresa's Will with the Surrogate's Court seeking to have it probated. Debra duly filed objections to the probate of Theresa's Will on the grounds that: (1) the Will was not properly witnessed, and (2) the Will is a product of undue influence because Ann, as attorney-drafter of the Will, also receives a bequest. Debra also asserts that she is entitled to the Big Bank account in the event the court admits the Will to probate.

Ann has opposed Debra's objections and has submitted proof of the relevant facts set forth above.

(a) How should the Surrogate's Court rule on Debra's objections to probate:
   (1) that the Will was not properly witnessed; and
   (2) that Ann, as the attorney-drafter and a beneficiary under the Will, exercised undue influence on Theresa in the execution of the Will?
(b) If the Will is admitted to probate, will Debra be entitled to receive:
   (1) the diamond ring; and
   (2) the proceeds of the Big Bank account?
(c) To what extent is Ann entitled to receive both Executrix's commissions and legal fees?

Actual Past Bar Exam Answer to Question 10

Score = 41.13

a.1. The will was not properly witnessed.

The issue is whether an interested witness can validly witness a will.

A valid will requires the testament to sign at the end of a written document, to publish the document as her will and to have two disinterested parties witness the will.

Debra and Jane were the witnesses to Theresa's will. Debra received a bequest (?) in the will so she is an interested party and cannot witness the will. If however, Debra can prove that she is an intestate distribute, her being an interested witness would be of no consequence since intestate distributes who have an interest in the will can validly witness the will. If not, Debra cannot witness the will, leaving only one valid witness to the will creating an invalid will. **(1)**

2. The issue is whether Ann will be presumed to have exercised undue influence on Theresa since Ann did not get Theresa's written acknowledgement to act as drafter, executrix & beneficiary under the will.

When an attorney drafts a will and the testater asks that the attorney be executrix a receive a bequest under the will, that attorney is required to advise the client (as Ann did here) that anyone can serve as executrix and that the attorney would be receiving additional compensation as executrix, beneficiary, and drafter of the will. In addition to orally advising client an attorney is required to get the testaters consent and acknowledgement of the forgoing in writing signed by testor. Ann may orally advised Theresa of all of the compensation Ann would be receiving. Without the signed writing a presumption of undue influence arises. **(2)**

Undue influence can arise when someone in a position of psychological dominance or fiduciary relationship coerces or influences a transaction with another in favor of the dominant psychological party. A special relationship must exist. Theresa was Ann's client which gives use to a fiduciary relationship where Ann has a duty of loyalty to Theresa. Having an interest in the will could have been a result of Theresa's friendship w/ Ann or Ann could have exerted pressure of Theresa unknowingly to Ann. Since there is no signed writing, and Ann's advice to Theresa being oral, the assumption of undue influence arises & it may not be rebutted by Ann w/o the writing. **(3)**

b.1. & 2. Debra will likely receive the diamond ring & the proceeds from the bank account.

Intestate succession provides that the next of kin of decedent is to receive personal & real property of decedent. If the court deems that the will was valid, Debra would get the bequest of the diamond ring. **(4)**

When a testator sells property bequeathed in a will, that is similar to relinquishing the bequest. The proceeds should go to residence of estate & pass to Gina since Theresa sold the painting and put the proceeds in a bank account help only by Theresa. **(5)** If the anti-lapse statute in controlling Theresa's issue or sibling (Dena) would receive a bequest that lapses such as the bank account. **(6)**

c. The issue is whether Ann is entitled to executrix and legal fees when there is no signed writing from Theresa acknowledging Ann advised Theresa of her rights.

Ann is not entitled to executrix & legal fees b/c she did not comply w/ the signed writing requirement and there is a presumption that Ann exercised undue influence over Theresa b/c there is not signed writing. **(7)**

Your Comments

(1) _____

_____

_____

(2) _____

_____

_____

(3) _____

_____

_____

(4) _____

_____

_____

(5) _____

_____

_____

(6) _____

_____

_____

(7) _____

_____

_____

Our Analysis

(1) First, this law is incorrect. The will is valid, but Debra will not receive her SHARE unless she would also receive an intestate share. Next, where is the conclusion? WILL Debra receive an intestate share? There is very little analysis here and the bar examiner is expected to fill in the blanks. Stay away from "ifs" — analyze the facts that you have.

(2) This all speaks to the issue of what an attorney can or cannot do, but what is the rule for undue influence? Yes, it appears in the next paragraph, but you do not want the bar examiners to think that you left it out. This is why organization is important. Remember to only address the question that is being asked of you, as you are limited for time. Also, the bar examiners want to make sure you can stick to the question at hand, as if you were advising a client on a particular issue.

(3) This paragraph is not very clear, and it lacks analysis. Also, the author seems to be mixing the rules of fiduciary duty and undue influence. We have said it before, but again, clearly lay out a rule, and then clearly apply the facts to that rule. Here, there is a rule laid out and a conclusion, but very little analysis.

(4) Be sure that your legal conclusions are consistent. We suggest using language such as "assuming the will is found valid" when you've previously concluded otherwise. The author previously concluded that the will was not valid because Debra was an interested witness, so there is a disconnect with Debra receiving the ring under the will.

(5) This paragraph should have more analysis. The important fact is that Theresa had a Picasso painting that was bequeathed to Debra. However, before she died, she sold the painting and deposited the proceeds from the sale in the bank account. The bar examiner wants to see that you've identified the issue that if a specific gift is sold during the testator's lifetime, the proceeds of that sale will go to the residue and the party who was supposed to receive the specific gift will not take. The author has the correct conclusion, but the bar examiner is required to fill in the blanks as to how the author got there.

(6) There seems to be too little analysis here.

(7) Where is there undue influence? Do not assume that the bar examiners can read your mind. Yes, they can read the fact pattern as well, and may come to their own conclusions, but the entire purpose of this exam is to show off what YOU, the examinee, know. To do that you have to apply the facts — whenever you make an assertion, such as "Ann exercised undue influence ..." explain why you think that. Here the examinee followed up with "because there is not a signed writing," but does that alone prove there is undue influence? Probably not. If the author was trying to follow an IRAC structure, as you can see, the author only has an Issue paragraph and a Conclusion paragraph, failing to include the most important paragraph — Analysis. If your answer is only one or two sentences, then it is probably not going to get you many points.

General Comments

This author did not use enough analysis throughout the essay and at times applied incorrect law.

General Comments on Essays That Receive Scores in the 40s

As you can see, many of the essays with scores in the 40s lack clear rules. They also often get the rules incorrect. Scores in the 40s will generally not get you to a passing score, so you can see the importance of knowing the law and expressing it clearly. In addition, many of the essays with scores in the 40s are poorly organized and structured, and lack analysis. You can see that we keep telling you that analysis is key, but the scores really do speak for themselves.

SOL/TORTS/NO FAULT INSURANCE *Question 1 Revisited*

Driver was traveling west on State Street at 35 miles per hour, the posted speed limit. He entered the intersection of State Street and Main Street without stopping or reducing his speed. Driver's vehicle struck broadside a car traveling southbound through the intersection on Main Street. Normally, a stop sign would have faced westbound traffic on State Street, but the night before vandals had stolen the stop sign. Driver was familiar with the intersection, but on this occasion did not observe that the stop sign normally controlling westbound traffic on State Street was not in place. There was no traffic control device for traffic proceeding southbound on Main Street.

Passenger was riding in Driver's vehicle. Although wearing a seat belt, she sustained a fracture to her right arm. Passenger was taken to the hospital following the collision.

Physician said that her broken arm did not require surgery and simply placed it in a cast. Three months later, on the day of her last visit to Physician, Passenger was advised that the fracture was not healing, so Passenger decided to change her care from Physician to Surgeon.

Surgeon told Passenger that the type of fracture which Passenger sustained should have been treated differently at the beginning so as to permit proper healing. Surgeon performed a surgical procedure, causing Passenger additional pain and suffering, but also permitting Passenger's fracture to properly heal.

Passenger retained Attorney to represent her interests in any claim against Driver and Physician. Passenger agreed to pay a contingent fee of 1/3 of the amount of any settlement or judgment obtained, after deduction of the expenses of litigation. No writing memorialized this agreement.

Two years and eight months after the accident, Attorney duly commenced an action on Passenger's behalf against Driver and Physician to recover damages for Passenger's pain and suffering. The complaint alleged negligence against Driver and malpractice against Physician.

In answering the complaint, Driver asserted that the accident was not his fault and was unavoidable, and in any event, that the non-healing of the fracture was not caused by the accident. Physician and Driver each raised an affirmative defense based on the statute of limitations.

(a) Was the action timely commenced against each defendant?

(b) Assuming the action was timely commenced as to Driver:

(1) Analyze the issues relating to the liability of Driver for Passenger's non-economic loss arising from the accident, including a discussion of the merits of Driver's defense that the accident was not his fault and was unavoidable; and

(2) Analyze the issues relating to the liability of Driver for Passenger's pain and suffering arising from Physician's alleged malpractice.

(c) Will Attorney be entitled to any legal fee for his work on behalf of Passenger if a settlement or judgment is obtained?

Actual Past Bar Exam Answer to Question 11

Score = 39.71

a. The issue is whether the Statute of Limitations has time barred the plaintiff from commencing an action against each defendant. **(1)**

For claims of medical malpractice, the statute of limitations is 2 years and six (6) months. Time begins to run on the date of injury, or in cases where the plaintiff is being continuously treated by the same physician for the injury from the accident, the date begins to run from the last day of treatment. **(2)**

It should be noted that the statute of limitations is a statutory requirement that restricts the amount of time a person has to bring a cause of action against an alleged wrongdoer. It is believed that people should not have to constantly be in fear of litigation for acts committed a long time ago. The running of time (or the end thereof) stops a plaintiff from bringing an action. **(3)**

In this case, the statutory time began to run when the plaintiff's cause of action arose. **(4)** For plaintiff passenger's claim against Driver, the time began to run on the date of the accident which immediately caused Passenger's broken arm. **(5)** For causes of action based on negligence, the statute of limitations is three (3) years. **(6)** Accordingly, passenger's cause of action will be invalid unless passenger initiates a lawsuit before three years from the date of the accident accrued. **(7)** Because it has only been 2 years and eight months since the accident, passenger's negligence claim against driver was timely commenced. **(8)**

Although the statute of limitations for cases of medical malpractice is 2 ½ (two and one half) years, the statute is tolled when the plaintiff is under the continuous treatment of the physician who treated the injury from the car accident. **(9)** Continuous treatment by the same physician, but for another ailment does not toll the statute. **(10)**

In this case, passenger's cause of action of medical malpractice against physician began to run three months after the accident since passenger was being continuously treated. **(11)**

Since it has only been 2 years and six (6) months from passenger's last date of treatment, passenger's action was timely commenced against physician.

b. 1. **(12)** The issue is whether Driver is liable for non-economic losses resulting from an accident that Driver alleges is not his fault and that the accident was unavoidable.

In New York, the no-fault insurance laws provide coverage for damages causes by the insured driver without regard to fault. The law was intended to encourage drivers to insure themselves and alleviate the amount of traffic accident cases that were clogging the court system.

The law, however, does not cover non-economic losses. Even if Driver was not insured, he is not liable for non-economic losses, even if Driver is found to be negligent and the accident avoidable. **(13)**

This accident could have clearly been avoidable if it were not for Driver's negligence. **(14)** Negligence requires a duty of care, a breach of that duty, which proximately caused another injury. **(15)**

In this case, Driver has a reasonable duty to drive safely. Since Driver was familiar with the intersection, he should have anticipated the stop sign and would notice the absence of it. Also, when making a turn into traffic, a driver has reasonable duty to slow down so as not to loss control of the car. Although Driver was not violating and speeding laws, he breached his duty by failing to stop at an intersection where it would be reasonable to know of the stop sign and its disappearance, as well as failing to reduce his speed when making a turn. **(16)**

Driver's breach of his duties ran to his passenger and other occupants of other vehicles, which was the proximate cause of passenger's injury. But for driver's negligence, passenger would not have been injured. **(17)**

b. 2. The issue is whether Driver will be liable for damages for pain and suffering of passenger. **(18)**

Comparison Notes

Some students may at this time choose to flip back to Answer 1, which received a 64.46, and compare that answer to the answer presented to the same fact pattern above.

Note to yourself the major difference between the answer in Question 1 and the answer given here. Take a few moments to jot down your thoughts and key differences here:

Answer 1	Answer 11
(1) _____	(1) _____
_____	_____
_____	_____
(2) _____	(2) _____
_____	_____
_____	_____
(3) _____	(3) _____
_____	_____
_____	_____
(4) _____	(4) _____
_____	_____
_____	_____
(5) _____	(5) _____
_____	_____
_____	_____
(6) _____	(6) _____
_____	_____
_____	_____

Our Analysis

(1) Overall, good issue statement, but we would suggest stating the two defendants, driver and physician, rather than just defendants.

(2) This rule statement is only half right. Because this question requires you to analyze two defendants, a driver and a physician, both Statutes of Limitations will apply, negligence statute of limitations and medical malpractice statute of limitations, and should be addressed in the rule.

(3) While this is not incorrect, it seems unnecessary. Remember you have limited time, and the examiners want you to get straight to the point.

Why is this relevant? It would be a nice addition for a law school exam, to let your professor know that you are aware of the policies behind the law, but here, on the bar exam, you just need to state the law.

(4) For the analysis section, it is better to use the facts of the case when you are applying the rule of law. Instead of saying "cause of action arose" say "when the plaintiff broke his arm in the car accident" since this is the point of time in the facts that began the clock for the SOL. Also, it is important to make a distinction between the cause of action against the doctor and one against the driver. The statute of limitations will be different for these defendants.

(5) This is a bit wordy but states the point of time in which the SOL starts. This sentence can be rewritten into the first statement.

(6) This statement should be stated in the author's RULE paragraph. It is confusing here because this contradicts what the author stated earlier. Are we dealing with medical malpractice or a tort claim? Two years and six months or three years? The examiners will accept differing outcomes, and often do, but you should always be clear and consistent. Lay out a CLEAR rule and apply it, and no matter what, do not contradict yourself.

(7) This sentence is unnecessary and not entirely correct as stated. SOL does not "invalidate" a suit, it is an affirmative defense.

(8) The author is discussing two defendants in this answer. However, that is not clear. Be sure that as an author, you are always making things clear. Split this into two parts if necessary.

(9) This is confusing and indicates to the examiners that you might not know what you are discussing. Tackle one issue, one defendant at a time. Also, since the author already discussed the rule in an earlier paragraph, this paragraph is repetitive.

(10) Does this rule apply to these facts? If so, how?

(11) What are the facts that support the conclusion that the plaintiff was being continuously treated? This paragraph should be the *analysis* paragraph, but the analysis is weak since it doesn't fully explain why the rule should be applied to these facts. **Avoid the pitfall of restating rules or conclusions as your analysis.** Instead use the facts to point out why the rules you use apply to the facts of the situation.

(12) Good set-up with subsections, etc. Organization is key, and the better you organize, the easier it is to read. Making your essay easy to read makes bar examiners happy. You want happy bar examiners.

(13) I'm very confused by this statement and I'm sure the bar examiners are, too. Be sure that you are always laying out a clear rule of law. Here, the first issue to be addressed was really as simple as negligence. As simple as it sounds, whether the driver was actually negligent should have been discussed first.

(14) This is a bit conclusory. The author has not yet laid out a rule or an analysis, or even told us that negligence was the issue.

(15) Here, the author states the rule of law, but is missing an important element that there must be "but for" causation in addition to proximate causation.

(16) This is all very unclear. It seems to me that the author is trying to state that the accident was foreseeable because of the stop sign but as you can see, the author never actually states this. Lay out a rule, then analyze that rule.

(17) We know where the author *wishes* to go with this paragraph—he intends to show there was negligence by stating the elements. However, as you can see, the author has made a few errors. First, the author's terminology is incorrect: "ran to his passenger and other occupants" makes no sense—duties don't "run to" others. This isn't a Property essay! He *owed* them a duty, clear and simple. The author already discussed breach in the above paragraph. Next, the "but for" and proximate causation sections are lacking analysis—the author is trying to *prove* negligence by stating that the "but for" cause *was* negligence—a BIG no-no. What the author probably meant was "but for the driver losing control of the car, passenger would not have been injured." Lastly, the author forgot an important element, the damage element of negligence. This is an example of something that seems obvious, but it is important to mention that the passenger was, in fact, injured to complete your negligence analysis.

(18) What happened? Where is the rest? One thing you do not want to do is not finish. Yet again, this is where outlining will save you, by helping you plan your time accordingly.

CORPORATIONS/ETHICS

Four years ago, Lawyer represented Client in the purchase of a house and in the preparation and execution of Client's will. Shortly thereafter, Client contacted Lawyer and asked Lawyer to represent Client, Sam and Tom in the formation of a corporation to operate a restaurant.

Client was to be the chef and general manager of the restaurant and Sam and Tom were each investors. Lawyer filed a certificate of incorporation with the New York Secretary of State, creating R Corp. Client, Sam and Tom were named initial directors.

At their organizational meeting, Client was elected president, secretary and treasurer, and Sam and Tom were elected vice-presidents. Client, Sam and Tom, the sole shareholders, were each issued 50 shares of R Corp. Sam and Tom each paid $50,000 for their shares. The consideration for Client's shares was his binding obligation to act as president of R Corp. and general manager of the restaurant for a period of one year, the agreed value of which was stated to be $50,000.

Lawyer prepared the minutes of the organizational meeting. Since that time, he has continued to represent R Corp. in various general corporate matters, including disputes with its landlord and vendors. When the corporation was formed, Sam and Tom orally agreed with Client that Client would be the chef of the restaurant at an annual salary of $60,000 for as long as Client is a shareholder in R Corp.

The restaurant was an immediate success and has been very profitable. Nevertheless, Sam and Tom have refused to vote to authorize any increase in Client's salary or any distribution of earnings to the shareholders.

Last week, at the annual meeting of directors of R Corp., with all directors present, Sam and Tom voted to oust Client as president, secretary and treasurer and to terminate his services as chef and general manager. They voted to elect Sam as president and Tom as secretary and treasurer and to hire Sam's son to be chef and general manager. Lawyer prepared the minutes for the meeting.

(1) Were Client's shares issued for proper consideration?
(2) Is the agreement regarding Client's employment as chef enforceable?

(3) Assuming Client's shares were properly issued, will Client likely be successful in a proceeding to dissolve R Corp.?

(4) Under what circumstances, if any, may Lawyer properly represent Client in a proceeding to dissolve R Corp.?

Actual Past Bar Exam Answer to Question 12

Score = 38.99

1. The issue is whether Client's promise to manager the corporation and be the chef was an adequate capital contribution. **(1)**

The rule is that each shareholder must contribute something of value in exchange for shares of the corporation. Contributing services to the corporation entitles the person to be adequately compensated as the services are adequate consideration. **(2)**

In this case, Client's contribution consisted of his professional services as manager and chef. All shareholders in the closely held corporation agreed that Client's services were valued at $50,000 annually. Client's consideration to the corporation was in exchange for a 1/3 interest in the corporation. **(3)**

Therefore, Client's obligation to be chef and manger of the corporation for one year is adequate consideration in exchange for his interest. **(4)**

2. The issue is whether adequate consideration was exchanged between Client and R Corp to form a valid, enforceable employment contract. **(5)**

To form a valid employment contract, the agreement must accompany an exchange of consideration between the parties. Consideration provides a benefit to one party at the detriment of the other contracting party. A shareholder is also entitled to consideration for his professional services rendered. **(6)**

In this case, Client's promise to be the chef was given in exchange for his valued salary being used as a capital contribution to the corporation. **(7)** As long as Client is adequately performing his services as chef and properly managing the corporation after the first year, the corporation is obligated to pay him $50,000 annually.

Therefore Client's employment agreement is enforceable and he can sue the corporation for unpaid services rendered.

3. The issue is whether a minority shareholder can successfully dissolve a closely held corporation.

Under the Business Corporations Law (BCL) of New York, a corporation may be dissolved upon a vote of the shareholders. The date that the corporation was formed will determine what type of vote is required to compel a dissolution. For corporations formed before February 22, 1998, a simple majority vote of the shareholders is required to dissolve the corporation. To hold the vote, a quorum must be called, consisting of a majority of the shareholders entitled to vote.

In this case, 2 out of 3 shareholders were present, which was enough to hold a vote. With regards to a minority shareholder, however, notice must be given to the dissenting minority shareholder. **(8)** Where the corporation has shares that are publicly traded, the minority dissenting shareholder can simply sell his interest on the open market. However, in a closely held corporation like R Corp, a minority shareholder does not have the ability to sell his interest to the public. The only option the shareholder has is to write the secretary of the corporation giving him notice of his dissent and then compel the corporation to buy his interest at fair market value. **(9)**

Therefore Client will not be successful in a dissolution proceeding because he lacks the votes necessary to pass a resolution dissolving the corporation. **(10)**

4. The issue is if Lawyer can represent adversarial parties to the same litigation.

The rule is that an attorney is to be a zealous advocate for his client. A lawyer cannot therefore represent adversarial parties because to advocate for one would cause a detriment to the other. Also, confidentiality between Lawyer and his clients would be jeopardized if Lawyer inappropriately used confidential information from one party to benefit the adversarial party.

In this case, Lawyer cannot adequately represent Client without breaching his ethical duty to zealously advocate for R Corp. Lawyer may try to cease representing R Corp. or delegating another lawyer in his firm to represent R Corp, but the situation would still not be within the Canons of Professional Conduct regarding prior clients.

Therefore Lawyer cannot represent Client in a proceeding to dissolve R Corp. **(11)**

Your Comments

(1) _____

_____

_____

(2) _____

_____

_____

(3) _____

_____

_____

(4) _____

_____

_____

(5) _____

_____

_____

(6) _____

_____

_____

(7) _____

_____

_____

(8) _____

_____

_____

(9) _____

_____

_____

(10) _____

_____

_____

(11) _____

_____

_____

Our Analysis

(1) Watch your wording. Here, the author meant "manage" not "manager." Just that one wrong word made the initial reading confusing. This is not how you want to start an essay.

(2) This sentence seems a bit awkward. The key is making things easy for the examiners to read, not more difficult.

(3) The last sentence is not clear. The author would have been more accurate if he stated "Client's **services**" instead of "**consideration.**" The services in exchange for the 1/3 interest is the consideration for the contract.

(4) This entire paragraph could use a bit more analysis, and a bit more rule explanation. The author should have included the rule about "adequate" consideration, that labor or services performed for the benefit of the corporation are considered valuable consideration in exchange for shares, prior to drawing this conclusion. Remember that you should be sure that you do not draw any conclusions that you did not already discuss.

(5) Why would the issue be consideration? Isn't salary normally rendered for services? The bigger issue is Statute of Frauds, which the author doesn't discuss. This author lost many points for not addressing the important issue.

(6) Why is the fact that he is a shareholder important here? If you are going to bring something like that up, please explain why; otherwise it is not always obvious why it is relevant.

(7) This is an excellent and clear statement, which would have been useful in the authors answer to subpart 1.

(8) The author should have discussed the rules of a dissenting shareholder. Here, the author jumps from discussing a shareholder who was *not present* at a vote to a shareholder who *dissents* at a vote.

(9) This does not seem relevant.

(10) This paragraph completely missed the issue. The issue is not whether a company can be dissolved, in general, as it is unlikely that if the minority shareholder is being oppressed that the company would be able to dissolve by normal means. The real issue is whether the shareholder has protections. Shareholders have litigation rights, such as direct suits or derivative suits.

(11) There is not enough information here.

TORTS

Bobby, age ten, attended Golden Sunshine Camp during the second week of July 2001. On the morning of July 10, the camp counselors decided not to postpone a previously scheduled softball game for the campers despite the fact that the grassy field on which the game was to be played was wet from a recent heavy rain. When Bobby came to bat, he hit the ball past the outfield. As he was running between first base and second base, Bobby slipped on the wet grass, and he fell, sustaining a fracture of his left arm.

Don, a handyman at the camp, who had been watching the softball game, drove Bobby to a local emergency room for medical care. On the way to the hospital, Don said to Bobby that he told the camp director not to let the children play softball on the wet grass that day, because he thought someone might slip and get hurt.

At the time he registered his son for camp and paid the required fee, Bobby's father signed a form captioned "RELEASE," which provided, "It is hereby agreed that in consideration of the opportunity to participate in Golden Sunshine Camp (the Camp), I, as the parent of a camper, fully release and discharge the Camp of and from any and all potential liability to me or my child in the event my child is injured during the course of participation in any events held at the Camp."

1. **Can Bobby's father bring timely claims for his son for his injuries and for himself for medical expenses associated with the softball accident?**
2. **Assuming a claim can be timely asserted, and without regard to the release, provide a detailed analysis of the camp's potential liability.**
3. **Assuming Bobby is ruled competent to testify at trial, discuss the admissibility of his testimony regarding Don's statement.**
4. **Does the release signed at the time of registration bar any claims?**

Actual Past Bar Exam Answer to Question 13

Score = 37.79

THE ISSUE IS WHETHER BOBBY'S FATHER CAN SUE ON BEHALF OF BOBBY FOR HIS PERSONAL INJURIES? **(1)**

Under New York Tort law (NYTL), a Plaintiff (P) is entitle to recover for personal injuries against the tortfeasor once proved tortfeasor's negligence caused P's injuries. **(2)** In order to prove tortfeasor's liability under negligence theory however P must show that Defendant (D) owed P a duty of care, that a duty of care was breached (that D failed to act with the minimum standard of care a reasonable person under the same circumstances would have exercised), and causation, i.e., that the breach of D's duty was the actual cause of P's injury (that it caused P's harm). **(3)**

The facts here show that Camp (D) had a duty of care to Bobby because it was conferred the custody of Bobby for a week while Bobby attended Camp. The parents left the child to the care of Camp, and part of Camp's job and existence is to make sure that children under its supervision are kept safe. Therefore, Camp had a duty of care.

At this point the issue turns to WHETHER D WAS NEGLIENT IN ALLOWING THE GAME TO TAKE PLACE; OR WHETHER A REASONABLE PERSON UNDER THE SAME CIRCUNSTANCES WOULD HAVE TAKE THE SAME DECISION?

When the Camp decided to permit the soft ball game to go on despite the fact that filed was wet, after a heavy rain, which can surely imply the filed was very wet, and so it shows a huge likelihood **(4)** that the players could slip and that slipping could very well result in a injury, as here, a fracture. **(5)** A reasonable person under the same circumstances, an adult, as D, under his duty owed to those children and parents, is expected to act reasonably to prevent any foreseeable dangers from those under its care, and when D decided to allow P to play, Camp, breached its duty of care, proper conduct here was to postpone the game, in order to make sure that the children would not get hurt while playing. **(6)** The essence of softball game includes running, and it is obvious that anyone running in a wet grass is likely to fall if not certain to fall, and such a fall can result in injuries. **(7)**

In the same token, it is undisputable that because of D's breach of duty of care (but for D's breach), **(8)** P's fall result and he sustained a broken arm. If D had exercized care, the injuries to P would not have occurred and being under the direction of the Camp, the minor-P, follow its instructions and played the game, there was a trust from P and his parents on D to exercize the utmost care hwle in custody of the minor. **(9)**

WHETHER BOBBY'S FATHER CAN RECOVER ECONOMIC LOST RESULTED FROM HIS SON'S INJURIES? **(10)**

Under NYTL a P is entitled to money damages encountered in the process of recovering for personal injuries against the tortfeasor (s) to the extent necessary for such recover. **(11)**

Applying the facts, it is showed that Camp was negligent, and because Bobby's father can recover the amount of money it is necessary for medical expenses, hospital expenses, medicine, and other expenses related can recover for those expenses by timely suing (under NYCPLR personal injuries SOL is 3 years form the injury) D. **(12)** Regarding Booby's father action against D for the medical expenses associated to the injury, Bobby's father is entitle to recover those medical expenses necessary to Bobby's recover as well, because the father encounter such expenses as a result of D's negligent conduct.

Finally, under NYCPLR, parents of a minor are entitled to sue on behalf of their minor children whenever it is necessary. Under the circunstances, Bobby is a minor (under 18 years of age) an dit is proper for his parent (father) to sue in his behalf.

THE ISSUE IS WHAT WILL BE CAMP'S LIABILITIES? **(13)**

Camp as explained above will be liable for the personal injuires sustained by Bobby under negligence theory. Camp will be obligated to pay for Bobby's money damages which are associated to Bobby's recovery and it will also be liable for any pain and suffering if found that P sustained such injuries, and also for consequential damages if encountered.

A contract was formed because the parties entered into a bargained for an exchange (pay for Camp for the services and Camp performing the activities and care a summer camp provides). **(14)**

Under Contract law, Camp will still be liable for breach of contract, because Bobby is now stopped from enjoying most of the activities Camp offer, and also because D's breach of care owed to P and his parents now impairs the contract since Parents now have their purposes frustrate, noone would be obligate to leave the child in the Camp after it proving to do no be able to protect their child. Under the breach of contract theory, Camp would be obligate to return the money paid for the Camp to the extend not used and money damages if any encountered by the father, including consequential damages. **(15)**

Consequential damages may be shown by the fact that he parents might need to be home with the child, might need to hire someone to watch the child who now might be stopped from being involved in physical activities, remember that the family palns was to have Bobby in the Camp for one week, his injury occurred in the beginning of that time therefore those expenses could result from P's injury. **(16)**

WHETHER THE RELEASE AGREEMENT PRECLUDES FATHER'S CLAIM?

A caluse which excludes liability is enforceable if reasonable and not uncoscionable. Under NYTL however, a exclusionary clause under tort law is invalid if it releases the party form intentional tortuous conduct. Althout

D's actions are negligent, and not intentional, under the facts it can be clearly inferred that the caluse became unconscionable (unfair) because father consented to 'accidents' which any parent would correctly infer the result of fatality, and not resulted from a negligent act of Camp. **(17)**

Therefore, the clause is shown do not protect D from its liability because it unconscionable once it exceed the reasonable scope of the clause because father consented to release Camp for accidents and not for negligent conduct which result in his child injury.

Your Comments

(1) _____

_____

_____

(2) _____

_____

_____

(3) _____

_____

_____

(4) _____

_____

_____

(5) _____

_____

_____

(6) _____

_____

_____

(7) _____

_____

_____

(8) _____

_____

_____

(9) _____

_____

_____

(10) _____

_____

_____

(11) _____

_____

_____

(12) _____

_____

_____

(13) _____

_____

_____

(14) _____

_____

_____

(15) _____

_____

_____

(16) _____

_____

_____

(17) _____

_____

_____

Our Analysis

(1) You have been given a way to organize this essay. Use that numbering system and make it clear when you are going from one question to another.

(2) The author is attempting to give a standard for negligence. However, the question is really about the statute of limitations. ONLY answer what the very specific question is asking.

(3) Even assuming this was a negligence question, the analysis is poor. First, injuries are an element of negligence, so the author is incorrect to state that a P can recover if "proved tortfeasor's negligence caused P's injuries." Second, a person is not a tortfeasor BEFORE it's been proven that the person committed a tort (that's the same as calling a person a murderer before he has been found guilty—well, at least in the legal sense). Third, the author forgot to include proximate cause in his rule.

(4) Avoid words like "huge" and "totally," which make you sound 15. And well, unless you are a prodigy, no one wants a 15-year-old lawyer.

(5) Probably the author here is trying to show a breach of duty. However, that is not clear.

(6) Not only is this sentence hard to read, but the author is combining duty and breach. Take one element of the rule at a time, and fully analyze it before moving on. Also, watch your grammar and avoid run-on sentences.

(7) Again, the author is probably trying to discuss foreseeability here, but he doesn't make that clear. This is a perfect example of why outlining is key. Do not write your essays in stream-of-consciousness style; think about what you want to write, put it in an organized and coherent fashion, taking each element one at a time, and THEN start writing.

(8) Avoid using parentheses to analyze. If something is not important enough to be in the normal course of a paragraph, it's not important enough to be in the essay.

(9) The fact that the plaintiff was in the custody of the camp is more likely to be important to duty, not causation.

(10) Again, organize the essay the way the question dictates it be organized.

(11) There needs to be a rule here. This is not enough for a rule statement.

(12) I'm not entirely sure what the examinee is trying to say here. Please be very clear.

(13) This is where negligence should have been addressed, not in the first section.

(14) Why is it important to bring in contract law? This is why it is important to read the call of the question prior to writing. Here, it's the second question (not the first) that requires a negligence analysis. This question should have analyzed the negligence of the counselors and the vicarious liability of the camp.

(15) It is not clear to me what the author is trying to say in this paragraph; in truth, it seems that the author himself doesn't know what he is trying to say. Outlining will help you avoid incoherent rambling.

(16) All of this goes off onto an unnecessary tangent. The question doesn't ask anything about a contract. Stick to what the question is asking.

(17) This does not fully make sense. First, the author applies an incorrect standard of law. While we know that sometimes you may forget a rule or an exception, and that's okay, it is always important to be clear and concise to avoid losing any precious points. First, lay out the issue. Here the issue is "whether the clause excludes liability." Next, lay out a rule. Then, start the analysis. Why would this be unconscionable in this situation? It cannot clearly be inferred that the agreement is unconscionable, especially when the author laid out a rule that stated it is invalid if the party commits an intentional tort, and then further states that negligence is, in fact, not an intentional tort. The conclusion as stated is contradictory—this is why analysis is necessary.

General Comments

Many traps that cause bar examinees to lose points typically have nothing to do with their knowledge of the law. Reading the call of the question and subparts first will help set the examinee on the proper path in his answer. Poor structure and grammatical errors are distracting and can frustrate the examiner who is grading the essay. Substantive knowledge of the law is important but it is equally important to practice how to clearly lay out the substantive knowledge into a well-structured essay.

General Comments on Essays That Receive Scores in the 30s

As you can see, in general the essays receiving scores in the 30s lacked an organizational structure. The examinees most likely lost a lot of points because their answers were not well organized, were often unclear or needlessly wordy, and lacked analysis of the issue. These examinees discussed irrelevant rules or used incorrect standards of law. We know you think outlining is a waste of time, but so is being wordy or discussing irrelevant law!

CORPORATIONS

In April 2004, Main Corp., a New York corporation engaged in the manufacturing of shoes, formed a subsidiary corporation, Sub Corp., and transferred to Sub Corp. title to Blackacre, in exchange for a $1,000,000 purchase money mortgage. Blackacre, a commercial building located in Westchester County, was occupied solely by Main Corp. Tom and Jerry were the officers, directors and sole shareholders of both Main Corp. and Sub Corp. The corporations maintained separate business records and bank accounts. Sub Corp. had no employees, held no board meetings, and had no letterhead.

In June 2004, Main Corp. vacated Blackacre, and Sub Corp. entered in a written agreement with Amy, a duly licensed real estate broker, to sell Blackacre. The contract set forth in pertinent part that if Amy procured a purchaser for Blackacre, Amy would be entitled to a 6% commission upon closing of title, but that if Sub Corp. found a purchaser on its own, no commission would be due to Amy. On the day the brokerage contract was signed, Tom orally agreed with Amy that even if Sub Corp. found a purchaser for Blackacre, Amy would be entitled to a 2% commission on the sale.

Over the summer, Amy spent at least 100 hours trying to procure a purchaser for Blackacre, but was unable to do so. In October 2004, Amy advised Tom that she had found a buyer ready, willing and able to buy Blackacre for $1,000,000. However, Tom told her that he had already found a buyer, to whom Sub Corp. had sold Blackacre. When Amy demanded that Sub Corp. pay the 2% commission, Tom refused.

Amy hired Lawyer to sue both Sub Corp. and Main Corp. to recover her commission. The written and signed retainer agreement between Amy and Lawyer set forth in pertinent part that Lawyer would receive a nonrefundable retainer of $10,000 against a rate of $200 per hour. Lawyer duly commenced an action against Sub Corp. and Main Corp. asserting causes of action against both defendants for breach of contract, or in the alternative, for recovery under a theory of *quantum meruit*. In her complaint, Amy claimed, among other things, that (1) Main Corp. dominated Sub Corp. to such an extent that Main Corp. was the "alter ego" of Sub Corp. and was therefore liable under the contract as if it were a signatory, and that (2) the oral agreement between Tom and Amy was binding on both Sub Corp. and Main Corp.

Amy became dissatisfied with Lawyer's representation, discharged Lawyer and demanded the return of her $10,000 retainer. Lawyer refused on the ground that pursuant to the express terms of the agreement, the retainer was "nonrefundable." At the time of Lawyer's discharge, Lawyer had provided ten hours of legal services on Amy's behalf.

(1) **Can Amy's contract with Sub Corp. be enforced against Main Corp.?**
(2) **Can Amy recover against Sub Corp. (a) for breach of contract and/or (b) in *quantum meruit*?**
(3) **What are the ethical and monetary consequences of Lawyer's refusal to return the $10,000 retainer?**

Actual Past Bar Exam Answer to Question 14

Score = 26.87

A. WHETHER A **(1)**

THE ISSUE IS WHETHER A RETAINER IN A SERVICE CONTRACT IS REFUNDABLE? **(2)**

In a lawyer-client contract, a retainer clause is valid, however when service ends, lawyer is obligated to return the amount of the retainer deducted by any work performed by the attorney regardless of a non-refundable clause. **(3)**

Here the attorney worked for 10 hours and therefore client is entitled to the refund of the amount paid as a retainer diminished by the 10 hours of work already performed by the lawyer. **(4)**

Refusal by the attorney to do subject him to breach of contract damages for the amount paid less the service performed, any consequencial damages Plaintiff—client can prove, and mostly ethical punishment which could result in suspension of his license in the NY Bar Association and by another other Bar association attorney is licensed. **(5)**

Your Comments

(1) _____

_____

_____

(2) _____

_____

_____

(3) _____

_____

_____

(4) _____

_____

_____

(5) _____

_____

_____

Our Analysis

(1) This is incomplete. Be careful how you set up your essay. One great way to set up a bar essay is to number your answers to match the questions being asked.

(2) This isn't actually answering the first question, which deals with Amy and Sub Corp., not the attorney. Be careful that you answer the questions as they are asked.

(3) The way this is worded is a bit confusing. You want to first clearly lay out the rule — "are retainers valid, and when?" THEN apply the rule. Are there any exceptions to the rule? Are there times when retainers do NOT need to be reimbursed, such as availability retainers? Does that apply here?

(4) This is a good analysis!

(5) Again, this sentence is a bit confusing and deals with a breach of contract theory and ethical punishment. Even if your English language skills are not strong, practice writing more and more essays until you are comfortable, not just with the law, but with writing. In addition, the writer here brought up breach, but why? Did they establish a contract? The issue is whether the amount should be refunded, so there is no need to discuss breach. Also, the ethical considerations are good to bring up, but the author does not go into enough analysis here. If you state a conclusion be sure you are explaining WHY you reached that conclusion.

General Comments

This received a low score, because although the examinee used good law, and came to the right conclusion, he did not (1) finish his essay (which is ALWAYS important) and (2) he did not have enough organization and analysis. You will hear this from us a thousand times, but when writing an essay you must clearly lay out the rule, and any explanation or exceptions. Then CLEARLY apply the facts to the rule. It's simple — and why would you make things more complicated than they are?

MPT—IN RE LISA PEEL

[Evaluated In Question 17 As Well]

Applicant's law firm represents Lisa Peel, a private citizen who operates an Internet blog on which she posts news stories about local government, as well as movie reviews and items about her family activities. Following her post about a local school official taking $10,000 in audiovisual equipment for personal use, the district attorney subpoenaed Peel to testify before the grand jury and to produce all of her interview notes in an effort to get her to reveal the identity of the sources for her story. Peel seeks the law firm's advice on whether she can resist the subpoena. Applicant's task is to draft a memorandum analyzing whether Peel would be considered a "reporter" under the Franklin Reporter Shield Act, and therefore be protected from being compelled to reveal her confidential sources. The File contains the instructional memorandum from the supervising partner, the transcript of the client interview, a copy of Peel's school-corruption post, a copy of the subpoena, and a news article about the development of blogs as the newest form of journalism. The Library contains excerpts from the Franklin Reporter Shield Act, various dictionary definitions, and two cases.

Actual Past Bar Exam Answer to Question 15

Score = 50.21

From: Bar Candidate
To: Henry Black
Re: Peel Subpoena
Date: 26 February 2008

Please be reminded that I was asked by you to research some matters with respect to our client, Ms. Lisa Peel, and whether we can use FRSA to move to quash Peel's subpoena. After some preliminary research, I have discovered that we should be able to quash the subpoena, more specifically, she should be designated as a reporter under the Franklin Reporter Shield Act, and to be protected by said Act. **(1)**

Ms. List Peel should be classified as a reporter with respect to the FRSA. **(2)**

Under §901 of the Franklin Report Shield Act, a "reporter" means any person regularly engaged in collecting, writing, or editing news for publication through a news medium. **(3)**

In the case In Re Bellows, it was held that photographers, who are held to being regularly engaged in the gathering or assembling of news, and that their activities fall within the statutory meaning of "collecting" news for publication, should be extended the protection of the FRSA. **(4)**

Here, we could argue **(5)** that Ms. Peel should be protected under the laws of FRSA, because even though she is not technically a reporter, (meaning that is not her profession, and she even mentions that it is her hobby in our interview with her), **(6)** like the photographer in In Re Bellows, she should be afforded the protection of the FRSA because like photographers, Ms. Peel "collected, brought together, gathered, assembled" in her blog, daily events within Greenville. Further, the term collecting was fully defined by FRSA and alluded to in In Re Bellows. **(7)**

Further, it was noted that where the legislature has not defined a term, courts may use a dictionary to assist in determining the plain and ordinary meaning. As per Merriam Webster's Collegiate Dictionary 720, it defines reporter as a "writer, investigator, or presenter of news stories; a person who is authorized to write and issue official accounts of judicial or legislature proceedings.

At the case at bar, we can argue that even though Ms. Peel was not a reporter by profession, the fact that she is a writer, investigator, and presenter" of news stories should along be enough to grant her reporter status and to be able to quash the subpoena by implementing the FRSA. **(8)**

As per Ms. Peel, we could argue that she attends public meetings, makes calls to officials, makes comments all fit within the purview of what a reporter does and should be protected by the FRSA. In that the computer is being used as a way to report the news, the fact that we are in 2008 should make the public aware that it is just another medium to report the news. As per §901(6) a "news medium" means any newspaper magazine, or other similar medium issued at regular intervals and having a general circulation. **(9)**

Ms. Peel mentioned to us that her blog is updated every Friday, which can be viewed as a regular interval. **(10)** Moreover, the computer medium can be equated with a radio or television station.* **(11)**

However, Ms. Peel may not be afforded the protection of the FRSA, due to the fact that her blog may not be construed as "news".

The Columbia Supreme Court rejected an argument that messages posted on a "blog" could be construed as "news" or as being published at regular intervals. Hausch v. Vaughan (Col. Sup. Ct. 1995). It may be argued that Ms. Peel's blog, since she updates it only 1 time a week, is not "regular enough," so as to constitute newsworthy media. **(12)**

*It should be further noted that we can classify Ms. Peel as a freelance writing, who feels compelled to share with her community what is happening. With respect to the FRSA protection, the Franklin Sup. Ct. did grant it to a freelance writer for a magazine, in Kaiser v. Currie (Fr. Sup. Ct. 2004), and to an author or a medical article, Hullinell v. Anderson (Fr. Sup. 2002). **(13)** We can further argue that Ms. Peel is a freelance worker who works when she wants, and does not have a set schedule. She should not be denied the protection of FRSA because she did not have a set schedule. Further, one can argue that Ms. Peel had the intent to educate the public, and intended to let the public know what is happening in their community. Following the reasoning in In Re Bellows (Fr. Ct. of Appeals 2005), if a person has the intent to educate the public, said individual should be afforded the privilege of the FRSA, since it can be found that Ms. Peel gathered news for publication. **(14)**

If all else fails, we should be able to make a public policy argument. If a person is not able to express, through print, media, radio, tv, or now, in 2008, what is newsworthy to the public, it would leave journalists and reporters second guessing about what they should be saying and what they should be keeping "under wraps." **(15)**

Your Comments

(1) _____

_____

_____

(2) _____

_____

_____

(3) _____

_____

_____

(4) _____

_____

_____

(5) _____

_____

_____

(6) _____

_____

_____

(7) _____

_____

_____

(8) _____

_____

_____

(9) _____

_____

_____

(10) _____

_____

_____

(11) _____

_____

_____

(12) _____

_____

_____

(13) _____

_____

_____

(14) _____

_____

_____

(15) _____

_____

_____

Our Analysis

(1) This is a better introduction than the first sentence in the paragraph: "Please be reminded that I was asked by you" is a little informal for a memo to an attorney; keep in mind you are addressing your superior.

(2) This is divided by the issues, rather than case law, which is preferable.

(3) This is a good statement of the statute. This is also a good place to start, as the language of the statute is always the best source of the rule of law.

(4) This is a good example of briefly explaining the facts of a cited case.

(5) Be a bit more formal, for example, "it could be argued."

(6) Try to avoid using parentheses in this manner. This is part of the author's analysis, which is crucial to the memo and should not be treated as secondary information.

(7) This is a good beginning of an analysis. However, the last sentence is not ideal, because it brings up something as fully defined by FRSA, but the author has not yet told us what that definition is.

(8) Good conclusion. But WHY? What is she doing that makes her a writer, investigator, and presenter? This means something as simple as "when she collects information for her blog…" Be careful not to state a conclusion without proper analysis.

(9) Even though the sentence structure could be cleaner, this is a good analysis because it applies the facts of the case with existing law.

(10) Even if this is a quick reference back to the quoted statute, it is always necessary to explain why a fact is relevant — for instance, "at regular intervals, which meets the requirement of the above-stated statute."

(11) Yes, good example of using the facts, but where does it say a radio or television station falls under the purview of this statute? This author is doing a great job of bringing in facts, but he does not always completely explain the rule first, which is necessary. General note regarding asterisks — try to avoid them whenever possible! A good outline prior to writing will help ensure that you include everything you want to say *within* the paragraph.

(12) This is interesting, and we want to read more. What was going on in *Hausch*? What kind of reporter? Compare that to our case.

(13) Good use of fact comparison.

(14) Good, but place the rule before the analysis.

(15) Good to bring this in.

General Comments

Overall, this is a good essay, as evidenced by the score. Remember, the bar exam is a points game and you want to maximize your points whenever possible. Analysis is crucial in any essay, but there are other simple things you can do to write a better essay. Outlining will help you organize and structure your essay, grammar is always important, and remember who the audience of your memo is.

MPT – ACME RESOURCES, INC. v. ROBERT BLACK HAWK ET AL.

Applicant's law firm represents Robert Black Hawk and other members of the Black Eagle Tribe who have sued Acme Resources, Inc., a mining company, in tribal court seeking to recover for damage caused by Acme's mining coal bed methane from under reservation land, in addition to an injunction ordering Acme to cease its mining activities. The Tribe members claim that their water wells are running dry, leaving them without water for livestock and crops, because Acme's mining activities are depleting the water table. Acme's answer to the tribal court complaint denies liability for the alleged harm and also denies that the tribal court has jurisdiction in this matter. Subsequently, Acme filed suit in federal court requesting a declaratory judgment that the tribal court lacks jurisdiction over Acme and seeking an injunction against the tribe members' prosecution of the tribal court action. Applicants are asked to draft the argument section of a brief in support of a motion for summary judgment in the federal action or, in the alternative, to dismiss or stay the action on the grounds that the tribal court has jurisdiction and that Acme has failed to exhaust its tribal court remedies before pursuing its complaint in federal court. The File contains an instructional memorandum, a transcript of a client interview, a copy of Acme's complaint filed in U.S. District Court, a draft motion for summary judgment or, in the alternative, to dismiss or stay, and affidavits from a tribe member and a geologist. The Library contains excerpts from the tribe's constitution and tribal code and one case.

Actual Past Bar Exam Answer to Question 16

Score = 47.23

In the United States District Court

For the district of Franklin

Acme Resources, Inc., Plaintiff   Case No. CV 103-07

	Motion for
v.	Summary Judgment,
	or to stay or dismiss

Robert Black Hawk, et al,
        Defendants

The above named defendants move the court as follows: **(1)**

1. To grant the above named defendants summary judgment on the ground that there exists no genuine issue of material fact that the Black Eagle Tribal Court has jurisdiction over plaintiff Acme Resources, Inc., and the action pending before it under Montana v. United States (U.S. 1981). And that the defendants are entitled to judgment as a matter of law; or, in the alternative,

2. To dismiss or stay this action on the ground that Acme has failed to exhaust its remedies in the Black Eagle Tribal Court as required by National Farmers Union Inc. Cos. V. Crow Tribe (U.S. 1985).

This motion is supposed by the affidavits of Robert Black Hawk and Jesse Bellingham, the pleadings on file, and a brief filed contemporaneously herewith.

Dated: July 24, 2007

Respectfully submitted,

_____

Conrad Williams

Franklin Bar #1779

Counsel for Defendants

1. Plaintiff's argument disputing Black Eagle Tribal Court's jurisdiction does not raise a genuine issue of material fact and therefore defendants should be awarded summary judgment.

Black Eagle Tribal Court has jurisdiction over Acme, a non-Indian, because Acme has entered into a consensual relationship with the Tribe through its commercial contract allowing Acme to extract and develop a coal bed methane field under the Reservation. **(2)**

Pursuant to Montana v. Untied States (U.S. 1981), the inherent sovereign powers of a Tribe do not generally extend to activities of non-members of the tribe. Two instances exist where the Tribe may exercise such sovereignty. First, a tribal court can properly obtain jurisdiction over a non-Indian where the non-Indian has engaged in a consensual relationship with the tribe. Second, a tribe also retains jurisdiction over the conduct of nonmembers when that conduct threatens or has some direct effect on the … economic security, or the health and welfare of the tribe. **(3)**

Acme has entered into commercial dealings with the tribe by contracting with the Tribe to develop a coal bed methane field. This relationship resulted in Acme's conduct clearly effected the economic security of the tribe. This nonmember conduct has resulted in water wells running dry, depriving tribal members of their economic security, specifically the ability to grow crops and feed cattle. **(4)**

Because Acme fulfilled both exceptions to the general rule, the Tribal Court has proper jurisdiction over the company, thus depriving Acme of its only defense to the action. Since Acme has not disputed any other fact or issue of the case at hand, summary judgment is a property result. **(5)**

Because plaintiff Acme has explicitly violated Black Eagle Tribal Code §23-5 by degrading the environment of the reservation through its mineral extraction Defendants are entitled to a judgment as a matter of law. **(6)**

Tribal law prohibits conduct that pollutes or degrades the tribal environment. The actions of Acme have resulted in the diminishing water well supply and experts have determined that the water wells of the rest of the reservation will dry up unless Acme's conduct is ceased. Accordingly, defendants are suffering harm as a result of Acme's illegal activities. The spirit of the tribal Constitution seeks to preserve the reservation for the economic and environmental benefits of future generations. Allowing Acme to continue to degrade tribal land is in direct conflict with the tribal Constitution and the company's actions should be stopped. **(7)**

2. The action should be dismissed or stayed because Acme has not exhausted all its remedies available in Tribal Court and comity obligates the federal district court of Franklin to defer or dismiss pending the decision of the tribal court.

The pending federal court proceeding should be dismissed or stayed because the Tribal Court has yet to rule on whether it has jurisdiction over Acme. Until the Tribal court has decided such, the federal proceedings should defer the proceedings or dismiss the case without prejudice.

While the issue of the tribal court's ability to exercise jurisdiction over Acme is a federal question, the exhaustion of tribal court jurisdiction and remedies are subject to de novo review. Whether or not Acme is subject to tribal jurisdiction is still at issue and Acme's actions in federal district court are underripe. That is, Acme must exhaust its remedies in tribal court or obtain a finding of lack of jurisdiction in such court before Acme brings a federal suit raising a federal question. **(8)**

Your Comments

(1) _____

_____

_____

(2) _____

_____

_____

(3) _____

_____

_____

(4) _____

_____

_____

(5) _____

_____

_____

(6) _____

_____

_____

(7) _____

_____

_____

(8) _____

_____

_____

Our Analysis

(1) This is a good set-up. Because the purpose of the MPT is to have you do actual legal writing, you want to set the answer up as close to reality as you can within the confines of the exam.

(2) The author began the analysis without first explaining the rule. We would suggest moving this paragraph below the one following it—the below paragraph will set up the rule. This paragraph explains why the exception is applied. Also, be sure to pay attention to grammar. Acme "entered," not "has entered."

(3) Was this a direct quote? If so, be sure to use quotation marks. If not, we're not sure why the ellipses are in this sentence.

(4) Again, the author used "has entered" instead of "entered." While grammatical errors seem minor and even if the author is 100 percent correct with the law, grammatical errors can make an essay unclear or read awkwardly.

(5) Since the author used a case, Montana v. United States, to cite a rule, it would be appropriate to compare the current facts with the facts of *Montana*.

(6) Here, the author does not make it clear as to whether this is a new heading, a new rule, or part of an old rule.

(7) These are great, but tie them back into rule. Remember the purpose of any legal writing is not to explain what YOU know or think, but how the facts relate to the law. ALWAYS, ALWAYS, without exception, go back to the rule.

(8) Where is a rule to base this on? And where is the rest? It seems that this examinee lost points because, although the first part of the motion was relatively strong, the second part falls short, as if the examinee ran out of time.

General Comments

The author had some awkward sentences and his essays lacked structure. A good outline prior to writing will help ensure you discuss all the relevant issues and stay on track. Finally, while this is not an English test, grammar is important.

MPT—IN RE LISA PEEL *[Question 15 Revisited]*

Applicant's law firm represents Lisa Peel, a private citizen who operates an Internet blog on which she posts news stories about local government, as well as movie reviews and items about her family activities. Following her post about a local school official taking $10,000 in audio-visual equipment for personal use, the district attorney subpoenaed Peel to testify before the grand jury and to produce all of her interview notes in an effort to get her to reveal the identity of the sources for her story. Peel seeks the law firm's advice on whether she can resist the subpoena. Applicant's task is to draft a memorandum analyzing whether Peel would be considered a "reporter" under the Franklin Reporter Shield Act, and therefore be protected from being compelled to reveal her confidential sources. The File contains the instructional memorandum from the supervising partner, the transcript of the client interview, a copy of Peel's school-corruption post, a copy of the subpoena, and a news article about the development of blogs as the newest form of journalism. The Library contains excerpts from the Franklin Reporter Shield Act, various dictionary definitions, and two cases.

Actual Past Bar Exam Answer to Question 17

Score = 32.90

MEMO Re: Peel Subpoena

The following memorandum is intended to aid the firm in it's knowledge regarding subpoenas issued to bloggers and their validity. Arguments and statements are intended to present objectively the strengths and weaknesses of our client's effort to quash her subpoena. **(1)**

1. BLOGGERS and the FRSA A **(2)**

Pursuant to FRSA's preamble stating the Act's purpose of promoting the free-flow of information, subpoenas compelling reporters to disclose their sources of information are prohibited. There is a compelling argument for treating bloggers as reporters as both are collectors of information who express such information to the public. Out client's method of expression, publication of the blog on the internet, has yet to receive general community acceptance that includes a blog among traditional mediums of publication. **(3)**

It should be noted, however, that not many in the community of Greenville (about 10%) have used our client's blog as a source of information. Further, even though the blog can be printed and then distributed similar to a newspaper, most readers read blogs on a computer screen. Our client should consider the following positive and negative aspects of her situation: **(4)**

FRSA

FRSA's shows legislature's intent to make available more avenues of information. The prohibition regarding sources helps the client if FRSA is determined the be applicable to bloggers.

BELLOWS Case

2005 decision emphasizes the need to fully effectuate legislative intent and give reporters discretion. **(5)**

LANE v. TICHENOR

2003 case explaining statutory interpretation. Client could use case emphasis on "common characteristics" to analogize her blog and her activities as having common characteristic of providing information that may not always be available to general public or rural communities, which is also common of a traditional newscaster on television.

However, case also provides that when a statute spells out covered areas, it implies the exclusion of others. Client must overcome definition of "news medium," which did not include internet publication. **(6)**

CHANGING LANDSCAPE

Blogs and bloggers are new to the judicial arena. Depending on the judge, it is unknown whether reporter protections should expand to include new, variations of new reporting. **(7)**

Client should use television as an example. Before television, which were not easily accessible to most households, the newspaper and the radio were the main sources the public could use to know about current events. Once televisions, and newscasts on such become more common, broadcast journalists gained the respect that was given to traditional reporters. Reporters' right to not disclose identity and sources extended to broadcast journalists as well. Client's best argument for being seen as a traditional journalist reluctant to reveal her sources of information and not stifle the dissemination of news is the aforemention analogy. **(8)**

REQUESED ITEMS

Client should also consider merits of arguing inevitable discovery of that the DA's office has the power to subpoenaed information from the source itself without having to include client. She could explain that the DA's office could easily subpoena the persons named in client's blog and have those persons testify regarding the knowledge currently sought after. **(9)**

OBSTALES **(10)**

Because client and her blog are not subject to any editorial revision or comments, the DA's office will contend that our client could easily be spreading false information which could amount to a criminal offense. Without any "checks or balances" client is free to write and publish basically whatever she chooses. Requiring client to comply would not affect any of her free speech rights since the subpoena only seeks names and information.

To defeat this argument, client could use her past blogs to demonstrate that her main goal and general intent is to merely provide information to those readers who seek it out. Most of her blogs are very mundane information like schedules and minutes. Should client come across some personal or information that is to remain confidential, she should be able to use her own discretion, and not the Court's when she makes her decision.

It is shown from due research that client has legitimate arguments for using FRSA for her protection. **(11)**

Your Comments

(1) _____

_____

_____

(2) _____

_____

_____

(3) _____

_____

_____

(4) _____

_____

_____

(5) _____

_____

_____

(6) _____

_____

_____

(7) _____

_____

_____

(8) _____

_____

_____

(9) _____

_____

_____

(10) _____

_____

_____

(11) _____

_____

_____

Our Analysis

(1) An introductory paragraph should clearly identify what you will discuss in your memo. It is the first impression you will make on the examiner. When we read this introduction, we're not entirely sure what the purpose of this paragraph is. It does not help in answering the question presented, nor is it the traditional way to set up a memo.

(2) Memos should be organized according to the issues. The attorney requesting the memo does not want a summary of case law, but rather, an answer to his question. The examiners are looking for properly structured memos.

(3) While this gives us a general rule, it seems that the author is putting too much of his opinion into the rule. It is not the author's opinion that is important, but rather what the law supports. *Why* is there a compelling argument that bloggers should be treated as reporters? *What* arguments could be made for your client that she should be treated as a reporter?

(4) This paragraph is restating facts. Why does it matter how many people use the client's blog as a source of information? While it can be inferred that these facts weaken the client's case, this paragraph doesn't analyze why these facts are important or draw a conclusion. In addition, it is important to remember audience and tone — the client isn't going to "consider" anything about her "situation" — that's why she went to an attorney! It is the attorney reading the memo who will make a legal conclusion regarding the client's situation. It is perfectly acceptable, and actually encouraged, to bring facts in, but ONLY if you apply them to a rule!

(5) The author received a low score because he is just summarizing cases. Ideally, you want to organize based on issues and not only explain the rule, but also apply it to the fact pattern. When a senior partner, judge, or whomever, asks you to write a memo, she wants to understand how the law applies to her particular client. If all she wanted was a summary, she would not have to ask a fellow lawyer to draft a memo.

(6) Yet again, this does not get us any closer to understanding how the law applies to this particular case. The author takes a stab at it by saying that "client COULD use case emphasis," but we want to know more. Is that going to be successful? How does the current fact pattern apply to that case? Are the facts similar? What were the facts in *Lane*? Also, it is not up to the "Client" to determine how to use the cases — that is *your job* as an attorney. As always, remember that the purpose of the bar exam is to determine what kind of attorney you will be. The State of New York does not want to admit attorneys that charge clients, and then make the client do the work! Would YOU go to that attorney??!!

(7) This issue is why you are being asked to write a memo on the topic. Do not start with "it is unknown …" since you are being asked to resolve this issue, or at least offer an opinion about it, for a senior partner. By saying it is unknown, you are leading that partner to believe that you have not done your work.

(8) If this came from a case, it should be cited. This paragraph is conclusory and it is likely just the author's opinion. Your job in writing a memo is to take the current statute and case law, compare them to the facts of your case, and assist the attorney requesting the memo to draw a legal conclusion about the case. The examiners don't care about your opinion, but rather, what does case law support? It is crucial to compare and contrast facts in all the cases given and the current client fact pattern. Here, the author has yet to even tell us what the facts of any cases were!

(9) Why is any of this relevant? Is the opinion based on something? This could be a good argument for the client, but it would have to be based on existing case law. Remember that in a memo you need to *support* all conclusions with case law. Also, if the client was going to make the argument herself, she would not have hired an attorney.

(10) Be sure you spell things correctly, especially mainstream vocabulary. Also, keep in mind that the purpose of headings is to aid the reader—you would never label a heading as "Obstacles" in a memo.

(11) We understand that the student may have run out of time, but this sentence isn't really saying anything at all. The author should have left it out.

General Comments

In general, the author does nothing but give his opinion. You need to bring in the facts of the case, do some comparing and contrasting, and apply the current facts to the rules that the case law is giving you. Do not just give YOUR opinion, but rather, synthesize the opinions of the courts. The author probably did not outline the memo before writing. As you can see, there is no clear structure or organization to this memo. Outlining prior to writing will help you avoid the common pitfalls.

Conclusion

We really enjoyed writing this book. We know you already have the skills to pass the bar exam; we just wanted to find the most efficient and successful way for you to apply those skills. No matter what we have told you, we want you to rely on what you have seen in this book: actual graded bar exam answers. There is no better way to teach you how to write for the bar exam than to *show* you how it is done and what was achieved.

Now go out and pass the New York Bar Exam!